Undiscovered Islands of the Caribbean

Undiscovered Islands of the Caribbean

Second Edition

Burl Willes

John Muir Publications
Santa Fe, New Mexico

An RDR Syndicate Production
John Muir Publications, P.O. Box 613, Santa Fe, NM 87504

© 1988, 1990 by RDR Syndicate
Cover and maps © 1988, 1990 by John Muir Publications
All rights reserved. Published 1988. Second edition 1990
Printed in the United States of America

Second edition. Second printing July 1991

Library of Congress Cataloging-in-Publication Data
Willes, Burl, 1941-
    Undiscovered islands of the Caribbean / Burl Willes. — 2nd ed.
        p.   cm. — (JMP travel)
    ISBN 0-945465-55-6
    1. Hotels. taverns, etc.—Caribbean Area—Guide-books.
2. Caribbean Area—Description and travel—1981- —Guide-books.
3. Restaurants, lunch rooms, etc.—Caribbean Area—Guide-books.
I. Title. II. Series
TX907.5.C27W55   1990
647.9472901—dc20   90-5976
                                                           CIP

Design: Mary Shapiro
Illustrations: Vincent L. Costa
Cover and maps: Holly Wood
Typography: Copygraphics
Printer: McNaughton & Gunn

Distributed to the book trade by:
W. W. Norton & Company, Inc.
New York, New York

CONTENTS

CONTENTS

ACKNOWLEDGMENTS

This book would not have been possible without the expert help of gentle and intrepid travelers Robin and Derk Richardson. Thank you also to Peter Beren, Roger Rapoport, and the staff of John Muir Publications for their help. In this second edition, many thanks to Jane Phillips, Marie del Vecchio, Vincent Costa, Joe Tharp, and Connie Leong of the Cayman Islands Department of Tourism.

INTRODUCTION

The notion of a Caribbean vacation conjures up familiar images of St. Thomas, Jamaica, Puerto Rico, and Trinidad. There are, however, thousands of undiscovered islands in the Caribbean. Most of them are uninhabited. But between the well-known tourist spots—with their time-share condos, crowded beaches, and duty-free shopping—and the deserted, barren cays, dozens of secluded islands with friendly populations await the adventurous traveler. Although one can still find beauty and tranquillity on the larger and more popular islands, such undiscovered islands as Saba, Marie-Galante, Culebra, and the others described herein offer an escape to a seemingly bygone era, when the Caribbean was unspoiled by high-rise hotels, skyrocketing costs, ungainly crowds, and traffic jams. Many of these islands are rarely visited by more than a few dozen tourists at any one time. Some are so undiscovered that inhabitants of nearby islands may not even know whether they are populated.

All of these undiscovered islands are characterized by a quiet, unhurried life-style. On most, reasonably priced accommodations are available, the beaches are breathtaking and frequently empty, and the terrain is startling in its beauty, thick with green vegetation highlighted by brilliant blossoms. And as a rule, visitors are greeted by friendly local residents who welcome travelers into small guest houses and charming inns.

"So, you're going to reveal all these wonderful islands in your book and spoil them!" More than one friend expressed that reservation about this project. But most of these islands were selected not only because they are undiscovered but also because they are not especially vulnerable to rapid commercialization. A few require exceptional effort to reach, several have natural barriers to development, such as limited water supplies, and on others, the population has taken steps to preserve the land and wildlife from rampant exploitation.

Indeed, travelers who prefer to remain off the beaten track must be prepared to forgo such modern conveniences as perfect plumbing, air-conditioning, television, and easy access. Such precautions as reconfirming flights, taking carryon luggage, gathering maps, schedules, and explicit directions, and watching for hidden costs such as hotel taxes and service charges will often defer the difficulties.

Encountering the unexpected is what makes traveling to these islands so special. They are not booming tourist centers, opulently endowed with luxurious amenities. But they are full of marvelous surprises, from the natural splendor of the landscape, through the enduring reminders of the region's fascinating history, down to the intimate details of gracious hospitality.

Many of the islands encourage a certain amount of tourism; their populations depend on it to bolster the local economy and provide employment for members of the younger generations, who might otherwise migrate to larger islands. Moreover, travelers who are respectful of local values and customs can actually make valuable contributions to the island's economy and culture. On Carriacou, for instance, Andrew Young has restored a 300-year-old stone house for rental. A few more visitors would make it possible for him to plant his dream garden.

In this second edition we have added five more islands, all qualifying easily as undiscovered: three British Virgin Islands (Jost Van Dyke, Anegada, Guana) and two Cayman Islands (Little Cayman and Cayman Brac). Only Isla Mujeres perhaps merited deletion, with its "moderate" high-rise near the island's nicest beach. But we have received so many favorable comments about Isla Mujeres from readers and friends that we feel Arthur Frommer will forgive us for this one exception. The underwater park is spectacular, and life still moves slowly on this quiet Mexican island so close to frenetic Cancún. In Belize, Little Caye is no longer listed, as it is the private home of the Lomont family, who graciously accept adventurous guests on nearby Long Caye and North East Caye, the two most isolated and undiscovered islands in this book.

Lest the reader feel this book has exposed the last few undiscovered islands in the Caribbean, take comfort in the knowledge that only the most intrepid travelers tend to explore most of these hideaways, and that a handful of remote islands remain secluded even from these pages. So, as I learned on Union, in the Grenadines, walk softly, do not run through these undiscovered islands.

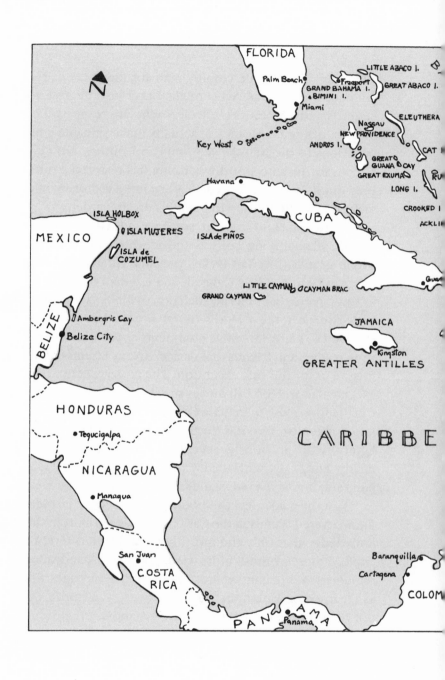

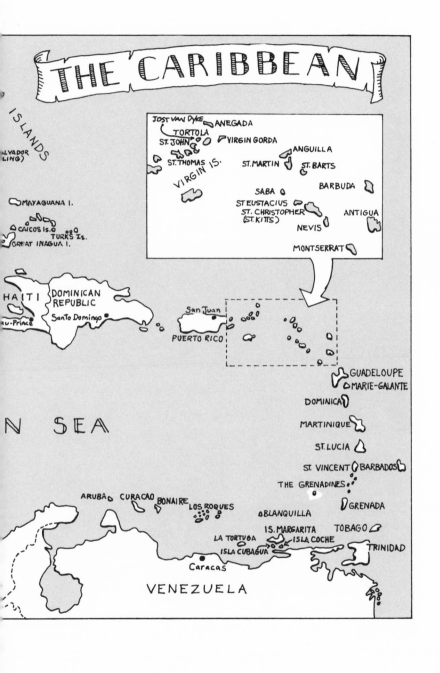

THE BAHAMAS

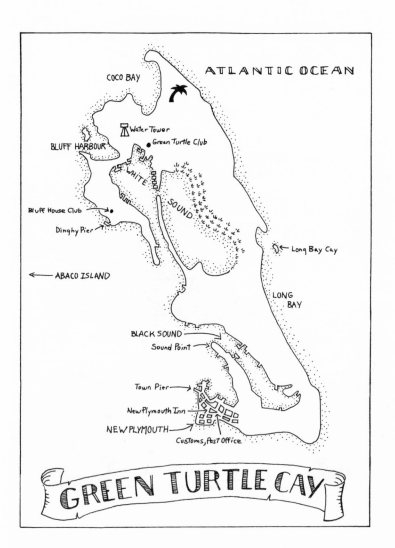

ATLANTIC OCEAN

COCO BAY

Water Tower

Green Turtle Club

BLUFF HARBOUR

WHITE SOUND

Bluff House Club

Dinghy Pier

ABACO ISLAND

Long Bay Cay

LONG BAY

BLACK SOUND

Sound Point

Town Pier

New Plymouth Inn

NEW PLYMOUTH

Customs, Post Office

GREEN TURTLE CAY

Green Turtle Cay, The Abacos

The Abacos, located just over 100 miles north of Nassau and 200 miles northeast of Miami, are gradually outgrowing their status as "out" or Family Islands in the Bahamas. Marsh Harbor, on Great Abaco, is a developed commercial center. Walker's Cay and Treasure Cay are luxury resort areas. But Green Turtle Cay, a short ferry ride from Treasure Cay, retains much of the charm of its late eighteenth-century origins, especially in its main settlement of New Plymouth, a storybook village with narrow streets and old New England-style clapboard buildings painted in bright whites and delicious pastels. New Plymouth provides a delightful trip back in time, while other aspects of Green Turtle Cay are perfect for the vacationer who wants to enjoy the water activities of the Bahamas without the high life of shopping and gambling.

Like much of the Abacos, Green Turtle Cay was settled in the late 1700s by British Loyalists who exiled themselves from the United States after the Revolutionary War. Descendants of the Loyalists and their slaves are the main inhabitants of the island today, where such family names as Lowe and Sawyer are still predominant. Again in the Abaco tradition, Green Turtle was once known for its fine boat building. Pineapple farming was also a major activity. But today, the restful island depends largely on fishing, services, and the small tourist trade.

New Plymouth is situated on a small peninsula with a main harbor at one end and the smaller ferry dock facing in on Black Sound. As we approached the town on the tiny Green Turtle Ferry, we could have been sailing into an old fishing village on the northeastern coast of colonial America. On every little immaculate street, hand-painted signs request "Keep GTC Clean," and people respond with a thoroughness that should leave any modern city dweller dumbfounded. A stroll through this genuinely quaint village takes you along tidy, paved streets that are essentially broad sidewalks, past the whitewashed picket fences that surround private gardens ablaze with colorful flowers, and neatly appointed houses with gaily painted dormers and gingerbread trim. Children, many of whom look very much alike because of the close family ties, ride by on bicycles. And a few tiny cars and minivans move slowly down the streets. The town includes several stores, a few restaurants, a fascinating museum, and a half-dozen churches representing several different denominations.

Much of the tourist trade is concentrated on White Sound, across the bay from New Plymouth, where the Green Turtle Club and Bluff House welcome the largest number of aquatically inclined guests. From New Plymouth, it is a short ride on the Green Turtle Ferry or a long, hot walk around Black Sound. But if you walk, you can take a side trip out to the ocean side of the island for the best shelling. (Note: if you walk, be sure to ask for specific directions to wherever you are going. And ask again until you are sure, for Green Turtle's roads branch off in many directions. We walked in circles on the way to Bluff House, ending up at the back of the Green Turtle Club three different times.) Brendal's Dive Shop (tel. 809-367-2572) is located right on the Green Turtle Club marina, offering equipment rentals, air fills, and scuba, snorkeling, and picnic trips. Just beyond the two resorts, crescent-shaped Coco Bay sits with calm shallow waters in a palm-lined cove.

Activity peaks on Green Turtle on New Year's Day, when locals celebrate the capture of "Bunce," a folkloric figure who hid in Abaco's forests; in May, during the annual fishing tournament; and during the week of July 4 for the sailing regatta. But for most of the year, the sense of harmony and well-being is undisturbed on this Bahamian Family Island. You step into a way of life that is determined not by the whims and fancies of high-rolling tourists but by the modest needs and traditional patterns of Green Turtle Cay's peaceful residents.

NOTEWORTHY

Miss Emily's Blue Bee Bar, in New Plymouth on Parliament Street, is famous for the Goombay Smash, a fruity rum drink that Miss Emily blends according to her own secret recipe. The simple two-room bar is the most popular watering hole in New Plymouth, and hundreds of off-islanders have left their business cards tacked to the walls. And the ice-cold Goombay Smash is as delicious and potent as Miss Emily is charming.

The Albert Lowe Museum is housed in a pretty, 150-year-old, green-trimmed white building near the New Plymouth Club and Inn. It is owned by Alton Lowe, a renowned Abaco painter whose work depicting the Abaco people and their way of life is featured on the island's stamps. Exhibits include artwork, shell collections, artifacts from the earliest days of settlement, and ship models built by Alton's father, Albert Lowe.

The Loyalist Memorial Sculpture Garden, across the street from the New Plymouth Club and Inn, was dedicated on November 14, 1987. It features twenty-four bronze busts of early Loyalists, arranged in the pattern of the Union Jack around a central pedestal with two female figures, one white and one black. The garden is testimony to the degree that this settlement reveres and stays close to its historical roots.

Rooster's Rest Pub and Restaurant, on a low hill on the outskirts of New Plymouth, is the hot spot on weekend nights. The local band, the Gully Roosters, plays Caribbean dance music, mostly soca and reggae, that keeps the spacious bar jumping with a large, integrated crowd of dancers. The energy of both the band and the patrons seems boundless, but anyone needing a breather steps out on the broad deck and rests beneath a black sky studded with millions of shimmering stars.

WHERE TO STAY

New Plymouth Club and Inn
Telephone: (809) 365-4161
If you have arranged ahead to stay at this charming antique

inn, Wally Davies will meet you at the ferry dock and transport you the two or three blocks in his electric golf cart. The eight rooms in the pink and white building are immaculate, with carpets, lace curtains, ceiling fans, and antique furniture. Wally and his wife Patty are gracious, but not doting, hosts. Wally's almost shy demeanor and wry sense of humor make him an unusual and ingratiating innkeeper. He and Patty preside over meals in the tastefully decorated dining area, which has a comfortable indoor room and a canvas-walled porch that extends toward the garden swimming pool. The dinners, featuring some elements of native cuisine, are prepared by Bahamian cooks. Rates are $100 double (plus hotel tax and service) including breakfast and dinner.

Harbour View Apartments
(formerly Sea Star Beach Cottages)
P.O. Box 282
Green Turtle Cay, Abaco, Bahamas
Telephone: (809) 365-4178
These simple beachfront cottages are tucked away in nineteen acres of coconut palms, citrus and banana trees, hibiscus and bougainvillea. Located one-half mile from New Plymouth by footpath, they rent for $70 for a one-bedroom ($450 per week), $75 for a two-bedroom cottage ($475 per week).

Green Turtle Club
Green Turtle Cay, Abaco, Bahamas
Telephone: (809) 367-2572
The hub of dive and sailing activity on Green Turtle Cay,

the sprawling club has twenty-four rooms scattered around gardenlike grounds. The knotty-pine dining room and richly decorated bar, festooned with hundreds of sailing flags, are focal points of social activity among tourists. Lunch—including conch burgers and fritters—is served on an attractive patio overlooking the marina. Rates start at $82 double.

Bluff House
Green Turtle Cay, Abaco, Bahamas
Telephone: (809) 367-2786
Bluff House commands the best hotel vista on Green Turtle Cay. Situated on the cay's highest point, a 100-foot knoll, the main house and dining room look out across the sound for a beautiful view of New Plymouth. Its cottages and condominium-style accommodations are arranged on the slope down toward a fine beach. Rates are $75 double, $85 for suites.

RESTAURANTS

At the Sea View, in "downtown" New Plymouth, Betty and Alphonso offer native Bahamian dishes and homemade pies. Dinner reservations required.

Plymouth Rock, near the main dock in New Plymouth, also serves Bahamian specialties and is open for breakfast, lunch, and dinner.

Laura's Snack Bar is a homey little hideaway on a back street behind the New Plymouth Inn. Formerly a cook at the Inn, Laura now prepares home-cooked specialties, including chicken and fish, peas 'n rice, coleslaw, macaroni salads, several kinds of pie, and homemade ice cream.

Rooster's Rest Pub and Restaurant offers lunches of conch, chicken, burgers, and various sandwiches.

FROM MY JOURNAL

A traveling Pentecostal crusade has set up its striped tent on the vacant corner lot across from the New Plymouth Inn. Only two dozen worshipers attend the Saturday night revival. More curious onlookers are standing around in the street. The village's established churches are holding their own services tonight as well, the sermons and choir music wafting from open windows on the warm night air. Walking down the dimly lit streets, we arrive at Miss Emily's Blue Bee Bar. Here's the action. We order our Goombay Smashes and continue walking under the moonlight. Over the hill, at Rooster's Rest, the crowd is feverish. Dancing to the Gully Roosters. We watch, dance, then step outside for air and watch the stars. We walk again, out along the still harbor and through the tranquil back streets of New Plymouth. Homemade ice cream at Laura's. It's wondrous that places like this even exist. The air is like velvet, the night is magical, the sense of peace carries us away.

HOW TO GET THERE

Direct flights daily from West Palm Beach, Ft. Lauderdale, and Miami via Piedmont Airlines and Aero Coach to Treasure Cay airstrip on Abaco Island. Green Turtle Cay is three miles from Abaco and is served by a water taxi that meets all flights on arrival and departure. The water taxi fare is approximately $12 per person round-trip.

Long Island

After you land at the Deadman's Cay airstrip on Long Island and pick up your luggage, you might find yourself all alone outside the matchbox airport, which is closed and locked up in a matter of minutes after the flight arrives. You quickly begin to sense the real barrenness and desolation connoted by the airfield's name. If you have not already made arrangements for ground transportation, a few taxis will usually be on hand outside. Before he leaves, the airport manager can also make the necessary phone calls for you. Most travelers come to visit the Stella Maris Inn at the northern end of Long Island. But if you land at Deadman's Cay, be prepared for a rugged two-hour ride over a road where the potholes rival the pavement for total space.

Long Island, located 150 miles south of Nassau, was called Yuma by the Arawak Indians and Fernandina by Columbus after he visited it in 1492. Life could not have been all that much quieter on these 400 square miles five centuries ago. Stretching ninety miles north to south, the island has supported sheep farming, salt extraction operations, fishing, agriculture (pineapples, bananas, papayas,

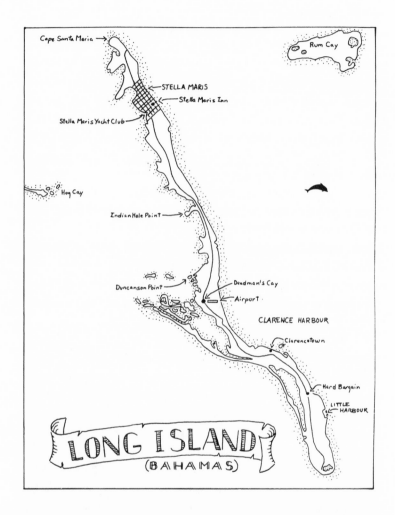

and corn), and boat building during its history. The largest segment of the 3,300 population lives near the middle of the island, in and around Deadman's Cay, which is adjoined by such settlements as Lower Deadman's Cay,

MacKenzie, Buckley's, Cartwright, and Mangrove Bush. The Government Road runs north through Salt Pond, locale of the annual Long Island Regatta, and Simms, an eighteenth-century seaport, to Stella Maris and Cape Santa Maria. To the south, the road leads to Clarence Town, the island's capital, the Public and Chancery ponds, Hard Bargain, and South End. The adventurous explorer who can withstand miles of bad road will be able to investigate dozens of old Anglican and Catholic churches, such as St. Joseph's near Salt Pond and St. Paul's and St. Peter's in Clarence Town. There are plantation ruins and attractive beaches in the southernmost reaches.

The western shores of Long Island, facing Exuma Sound, have the shallowest and gentlest waters, not unlike many coastlines in the Bahamas. But toward the northeast, the terrain is hilly, and the coastline is surprisingly rugged

and rocky. The waters here are especially good for scuba diving, with over twenty different spots identified for separate dives. With guidance from the dive masters at Stella Maris, you can even take a controlled dive to swim with the sharks at Shark Reef. Exploring colonial settlements that have changed slowly over time, enjoying the varied water sports and activities at Cape Santa Maria, and just getting away from nearly every sign of civilization are the reasons for a visit to this completely different sort of Long Island.

WHERE TO STAY

Stella Maris Inn and Estate
Box 105
Long Island, Bahamas
Telephone: (809) 336-2106
Fax: (305) 764-6651
Dominating the hills at the northern end of Long Island, this luxury resort sprawls out across acres and acres of scenic landscape dotted with coconut palms. Perhaps the effort required to get to Long Island deserves to be rewarded with a stay at this supremely attractive inn. Managed by two solicitous Germans, Peter Kuska and Jorg Friese, Stella Maris can accommodate 140 guests in a variety of rooms, cottages, townhouses, villas, and deluxe bungalows. There are three swimming pools on the vast grounds and six beaches within walking distance. Scuba diving is a specialty, and waterskiing and boat charters are available. The inn has its own airstrip, tennis courts, dining room, and coffee shop, plus a reciprocal arrangement with the Cape Santa Maria Beach Club nine miles away on the

powder-white sand of the Cape Santa Maria lagoon. Rates start at $70 single, $86 double for simple rooms and go up from there. Modified American Plan is available, as are package arrangements that include airfare and/or scuba diving and fishing. There is no charge for sailing, windsurfing, twice-weekly boat cruises, and tennis. Hotel provides direct air service from Ft. Lauderdale for $150 one way per person, $75 from Nassau and $40 from George Town.

J. B. Carroll's Guest House
Deadman's Cay, Long Island, Bahamas
Telephone: can be reached locally through Long Island operator.
For $40 a night, J. B. Carroll will put you up in one of the six bedrooms of his informal guest house, next to his market located on Government Road. He will pick you up at the airport if you call when you land and will rent you one of his cars or jeeps so you can explore the island. In the morning, he serves coffee in the dining room of his own house in back. The Carroll guest rooms are homey but very small and simple. They share three bathrooms. Around eleven o'clock at night, J. B. turns off his generator, so out go your lights and off goes the fan.

RESTAURANTS

Conchy's: Carole Archer cried for three months when her husband, Lamond (or "Lammy"), told her he was retiring from Xerox and they were moving from Nassau to Long Island. But in less than six months, she decided she loved

the remote island life. Now she helps Lammy run this small, homey restaurant just a mile or so south of Stella Maris. Lammy has committed himself to learning his native Bahamian cuisine and has mastered a variety of dishes. Proudly, he showed us his kitchen and let us sample the steamed turtle and the minced lobster. His touch is well worth the $8 to $12 for dinner.

Thompson Bay Inn: At Salt Pond, on the road between Deadman's Cay and Stella Maris, this modest restaurant bar serves excellent local seafood. If you call ahead, dinner will be ready when you arrive. We dropped in on our drive from Deadman's Cay to Stella Maris and returned to find a fresh, hearty meal waiting for us at the appointed time. The grouper and snapper are fried with native spices and served with spicy coleslaw, potato salad, and peas 'n rice. At about $6, dinner is a rare Bahamian bargain. Breakfasts are around $4, and fish or conch and chips snacks run about $3.50.

HOW TO GET THERE

Bahamasair flies from Nassau and Ft. Lauderdale, sometimes by way of George Town, Exuma, to Deadman's Cay.

The Exumas

During the drive from the tiny airport to the main settlement of George Town, Great Exuma, you begin to realize that having reached the Exumas, only forty miles southeast of Nassau, you are downshifting into the tranquil pace that continues to slow as you move south in the Bahamas. A taxi driver removes you from the momentary commotion that surrounds arrivals and departures at the airstrip and carries you the few miles to George Town, a one-road town that is a fascinating mix of grand public and rustic private buildings. Although the majority of accommodations are located here, the town has a pervasive sleepy feeling that is extremely conducive to worry-free relaxation and meditative strolls. Except in regatta and fishing contest seasons, this is as quickly as the pulse races in life in the Exumas.

The Exumas are comprised of some ninety miles of cays, with a population of 3,700. Most people live on Great and Little Exuma, with 800 "concentrated" in George Town. The islands' colonial history took its most significant turn in the late 1700s, when Denys Rolle took possession of 7,000 acres on Great Exuma, establishing five cotton plantations worked by his transplanted population of slaves. Cotton never really succeeded as a cash crop on Exuma, and Rolle's son, Lord John Rolle, presided over a failing empire until the emancipation of slaves in 1834. The Rolle land and name were subsequently passed down through the descendants of Rolle's slaves. Today, it is still the most prominent family name on Great Exuma. Jeremiah Rolle introduced tractor farming to the Exumas in the midtwentieth century, cultivating crops of giant sweet potatoes. When you land at the George Town airport, one

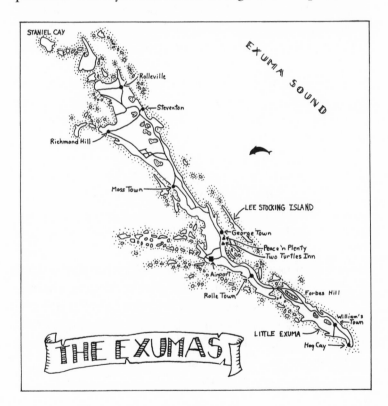

of the first things you see is the sign reading "Kermit's," marking the bar/restaurant of Kermit Rolle, one of the island's leading entrepreneurs who also owns the Hilltop Tavern in (where else but?) Rolleville.

The architecture of George Town, like most of the settlements in the Exumas, harkens back to earlier centuries and proudly displays the islanders' penchant for pastel paints, especially pink and yellow. In the bend where the road curves around the point of beautiful Elizabeth Harbour, an enormous, broad-reaching tree spreads its limbs above a small but lovely Straw Market, where a few local women display and sell their handcrafted hats, baskets, and other goods. Farther around the bend, past the impressive pink and white Government Administration Building and Hotel Peace and Plenty, the 150-year-old St. Andrew's Anglican Church faces west, its brilliant white walls and royal blue doors and shutters almost glowing in the bright afternoon sun.

By rented car or public bus, you can explore outward, north and south, from George Town. To the south is Rolle Town, with its old, vibrantly painted buildings and a small bridge that links Great Exuma to Little Exuma. The small town of The Ferry affords wonderful views of the sea and is the home of 70-year-old Gloria Patience, "the Shark Lady," who catches sharks, sells their meat, and makes jewelry from their teeth, for sale in her museumlike house. Just farther south you can look out over Pretty Molly Bay from the Sand Dollar Beach Club before proceeding to Williams Town, site of the Old Hermitage or "Cotton House," a nearly 200-year-old plantation estate. To the north of George Town, you drive through Jimmy Hill, notable for great expanses of deserted beach; Mt. Thompson, near a large bay with the shadeless white sand beach of Ocean Bight; and Steventon, before arriving at the charming hilltop village of Rolleville.

For snorkelers and divers, the Exumas offer a variety of underwater delights. The cays are surrounded by coral reefs at shallow and medium depths, and deeper wall diving reveals large formations of black coral. Blue holes, an uncharted Mystery Cave, and various banks and cays invite exploration. The diving facilities include Wendle McGregor's personable Exuma Divers and the larger-scale Exuma Aquatics, affiliated with Hotel Pieces of Eight. After taking some guests out for a morning dive, Wendle McGregor took us in his boat to a superb snorkeling spot among the coral reefs that lie at the distant mouth of Elizabeth Harbour. The scuba sites are abundant and the explorers few. Only in March and April, during the Cruising (or Crazy) Regatta and the Out Island Regatta, when festive visitors swamp George Town, is Great Exuma's languorous peace transformed into hectic plenty.

NOTEWORTHY

Stocking Island, about one mile offshore, protects Elizabeth Harbor from the Atlantic Ocean. Its miles of gorgeous, secluded beaches afford private sunbathing, excellent shelling, and marvelous swimming. (Some speculate that this may have been Christopher Columbus's first landing in the New World, a conjecture that San Salvadorans hotly dispute.) Its isolation and pristine beauty make it an ideal one-day escape into remote paradise. Boat transportation is available at Hotel Peace and Plenty for $5 (free to the hotel's guests).

WHERE TO STAY

Peace and Plenty
P.O. Box 55
George Town, Exuma, Bahamas
Telephone: (809) 336-2551; fax: (809) 336-2093
The oldest hotel in the Exumas, overlooking Elizabeth Harbour, was a sponge market until converted in the 1950s. Its distinctive pink-and-white painted buildings, with gabled roofs and dormer windows, add the charm needed to offset its size and tourist bustle. The popular hotel features thirty-two air-conditioned rooms (poolside, waterfront, or garden suites), a swimming pool, an attractive indoor-outdoor dining room, two cocktail lounges, twice-weekly dancing to live calypso, and courtesy boat transportation to Stocking Island. The lobby is a good place to glean information, from bulletin boards and staff, about what is happening in George Town. Rates are $72-$78 for a double in the summer; $98-$104 during winter. A new facility with sixteen rooms and a bar/restaurant has been constructed on the beach one mile away. It's called "Peace and Plenty West."

Two Turtles Inn
P.O. Box 51
George Town, Exuma, Bahamas
Telephone: (800) 336-2545

Located across the street from the Straw Market, near the bend in the road at Elizabeth Harbour, Two Turtles is a small, woodsy, twelve-room motel-style inn. The trade-offs for the clean but ordinary accommodations are the relatively reasonable rates and lively, informal atmosphere. Locals and tourists gather at the cozy bar and in the pleasant courtyard for often boisterous discussions of news and events. The sunken cavelike dining room, carved out of rock, serves excellent local seafood and native dishes for breakfast, lunch, and dinner, and the waitresses and cooks are very friendly. Some of the rooms are air-conditioned; all have ceiling fans and television. Rates are $48 summer, $60 winter, with four kitchenettes available at $55 and $70.

Pirate's Point Villas
P.O. Box 23
George Town, Exuma, Bahamas
No telephone.
Three comfortable housekeeping villas, located on a private beach; each rents for $70 a day.

Marshall's Guest House
P.O. Box 27
George Town, Exuma, Bahamas
Telephone: (809) 336-2081
These very simple island accommodations—twelve rooms in a plain building off the beach in town—are fine for the budget traveler at $22 single and $30 double.

RESTAURANTS

All the Great Exuma hotels have good restaurants that serve different combinations of Bahamian, American, and international cuisine in attractive dining areas. For very inexpensive home-cooked native meals, check out Liz n' Jim's, a tiny, weathered shanty in George Town. Darville's Supplies sells good homemade cakes and breads.

HOW TO GET THERE

Bahamasair has regularly scheduled service into George Town from Nassau. But be sure to recheck on all flights, as they are occasionally rerouted through Deadman's Cay depending on the number of potential passengers; or, as one woman put it, ''With this flight you take your chances. They should have told you.''

PRACTICAL TIPS

Immigration: U.S. citizens do not need a passport or visa to visit the Bahamas for periods not exceeding eight months; a birth certificate or voter registration card is accepted as proof of citizenship. There is a $5 airport departure tax.
    Currency: The Bahamian dollar is held on an exact par with the U.S. dollar. Both currencies are used throughout the Bahamas.

TURKS AND CAICOS

The Turks and Caicos have long been called the "forgotten islands." One hour and twenty minutes by jet southeast of Miami, this British Crown Colony consists of small islands with a total population of 9,000 citizens scattered among eight inhabited islands. Even with increasing development as a tourist destination, there is still about one mile of private beach for each inhabitant! Part of the Bahamas chain, the Turks and Caicos are flat islands with magnificent, empty beaches and the finest diving sites in the world. Inside the spectacular continuous coral reef, underwater visibility often reaches 200 feet.

The inhabited Caicos Islands include Providenciales (with direct air service to Miami), North Caicos, Middle Caicos, East Caicos, Pine Cay, and South Caicos. Across a 22-mile deep-water channel lie Grand Turk and Salt Cay in the Turks group.

Providenciales

O f all the Turks and Caicos islands, Providenciales
(known locally as "Provo") offers the visitor the
widest choice of hotel accommodations, restaurants, and
stores without spoiling its tranquil and friendly atmosphere. It is an island of peaceful rolling hills, a natural deep
harbor, flowering cactus, and a spectacular coral reef for
snorkeling, swimming, and diving. At Northwest Point, a
vertical drop-off to 6,000 feet is considered by experts to
be one of the finest diving sites in the world.

NOTEWORTHY

Social life on Provo centers around the church: the choirs
and the Church of God Band should not be missed. Church
services and singing last all day Sunday, and it is quite
acceptable to attend a service and leave at any time.

Scuba enthusiasts will head straight for Northwest
Point for some of the finest diving in the world, but the less
ambitious or experienced visitor can get a view of coral
and other marine life from the glass-bottom *Grouper
Snooper*, which operates regular boat excursions.

Caico Conch Farm: At the far eastern end of Provo, the world's first conch mariculture facility welcomes visitors. The distinctive glass-covered geodesic dome and large silver water tanks are easily recognized from land or sea. Inside, the fascinating farming of this fast-disappearing staple food takes place, from hatched conch eggs in controlled sea egg farms, to large larval tanks where they are fed and nurtured to maturity. The gift shop at the farm specializes in unique conch jewelry and rare conch pearls.

WHERE TO STAY

Although Barbara Francis, at the tourist bureau, said she could find "lodgin' with the locals," there are few bargains

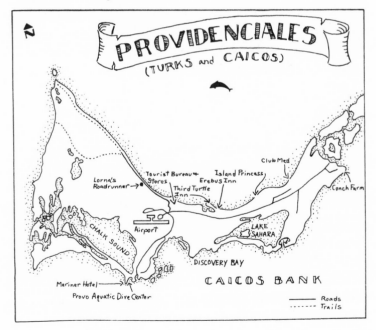

for the low-budget traveler on Provo. For the couple willing to pay at least $85 per night, there are several choices.

Island Princess Hotel
Reservations: Box 52-6002
Miami, FL 33152
Telephone: (809) 946-4260
Each room has its own veranda, ceiling fan, and big sliding glass windows. The beachfront location is ideal for families, and the general ambience is informal and friendly. The staff is extremely helpful and pleasant, and the dining room provides excellent food: local dishes, fresh fish, homemade breads. Complete watersport facilities are offered: windsurfing, diving, bonefishing, snorkeling. The dive shop is a full-service International Training Facility, and for the serious diver, Provo offers untouched underwater walls, gardens, reefs, and wrecks. $65 single, $85 double; special dive packages are available.

Mariner's Hotel
Sapodilla Point
Providenciales, Turks and Caicos,
British West Indies
Telephone: (809) 946-4488
Landscaped in a tropical setting, this immaculate 25-room hotel is located on a secluded and peaceful knoll just a three-minute walk to a fine beach and the Provo Aquatic Center (diving, sail, and motorboat rentals, windsurfer sailboards). Although I preferred the food at the Islander, the Mariner was my favorite room choice on Provo. Summer rates, $65 single, $75 for two; winter, $90 and $95.

Erebus Inn
Box 238
Providenciales, Turks and Caicos,
British West Indies
Telephone: (809) 946-4240
On a hillside overlooking Turtle Cove, a short walk to the
beach, shops, and restaurants, the Erebus has six rooms facing the marina, four individual bungalows, each with a
large balcony, and twenty-two spacious new rooms. Swimming pool, spa, air-conditioning, telephones. Rooms start
at $60 single, $70 for two; bungalows are $80 single, $90
for two.

RESTAURANTS

Island Princess Hotel has excellent buffet dinners with
fresh island produce, grilled or baked fish.

Henry's Roadrunner, Blue Hills, is a very casual local
restaurant, famous for its Wednesday night buffets, which
feature lobster, conch, grouper, barbecued ribs, turtle,
steaks, and red beans and rice. Reasonable.

Gilley's Cafe is a bar-restaurant at the airport, excellent
for lobster salad, lobster sandwiches, and homemade chili.

HOW TO GET THERE

There is nonstop service from Miami to Providenciales on
Pan American World Airways.

Pine Cay

Pine Cay is one of a chain of islets connecting Providenciales and North Caicos. Two miles long and covering 800 acres, it is a small, private residential community with a twelve-room hotel run as a nature preserve.

For the traveler who does not have to ask the price, the small and comfortable Meridian Club provides the ultimate escape from the rigors of the twentieth century. The two-mile beach is one of the finest in the Caribbean, and, of course, it is never crowded. There is a freshwater pool, tennis court, windsurfing, a nature trail featuring a wide variety of birds and plants, and outstanding snorkeling, diving, and fishing.

Rates start at $350 per couple and include three meals a day, free use of sailboats, bicycles, and snorkeling gear, boating excursions to neighboring islands, and free postage stamps! Closed August 1-November 1.

NOTEWORTHY

Fort George Cay National Park. Off the north coast of Pine Cay are ruins of a British fort. With the help of a local guide, traces of pre-Columbian settlements can be found in this unique park.

Water Cay and Little Water Cay. Off the south coast, these tiny islands are a shell collector's dream.

WHERE TO STAY

Meridian Club
Pine Cay
Turks and Caicos, British West Indies
Reservations: New York (212) 696-4566;
U.S. (800) 225-4255

RESTAURANTS

On Pine Cay, the only food available is served at your guest house or hotel.

HOW TO GET THERE

The hotel makes arrangements to meet you at the Providenciales airport for a short hop to the island.

North Caicos

Nature lovers will find an earthly paradise on North Caicos. This large and most northerly of the chain is also the most fertile. Limes, papayas, sapodillas, oranges, tamarinds, and grapefruit abound. Endless beautiful beaches ring the island. Charming villages, quiet walks, and unusual species of birds are among its wonders.

NOTEWORTHY

Flamingo Pond, to the south of Whitby, harbors a nesting place for exotic flamingos, now rare in the wild.

Bottle Creek Settlements. Six miles southeast of Whitby, this quiet settlement has changed little since the nineteenth century. Inhabitants live mainly off fresh fish, crayfish, and shellfish. Beautiful beaches offer long, solitary walks and swims in the crystal-clear water.

Four miles west of Whitby by boat, Three Mary Cays is a haven of unspoiled beauty, fine beaches, and clear water. There are limestone caves to explore on the north coast, and my favorite secluded beach is nearby at Mudjin Harbor.

WHERE TO STAY

Pelican Beach Hotel
North Caicos
Turks and Caicos, British West Indies
Telephone: (809) 946-7112
North Caicos native Clifford Gardiner owns and operates
this friendly twelve-room and two-suite hotel. Daily rate
starts at $50 per person and includes breakfast and dinner.
There are ten miles of uncrowded white sand beach at your
doorstep. Equipment is available for day sailing, snorkel-
ing, and scuba.

Prospect of Whitby Hotel
North Caicos
Turks and Caicos, British West Indies
Telephone: (809) 946-7119
Situated on a seven-mile-long stretch of beach, the Pros-
pect of Whitby Hotel provides a swimming pool, tennis,
dive shop, and water sports. Fresh produce comes from
their garden.

RESTAURANTS

On North Caicos, the only food available is served at your
guest house or hotel.

HOW TO GET THERE

There are daily 15-minute flights from Providenciales to
North Caicos on Turks and Caicos National Air.

Middle Caicos

With a population of only 1,000 residents, Grand Caicos, or Middle Caicos, as it is often called, is the largest and least developed of any of the inhabited Turks and Caicos. This attractive island, with magnificent beaches and beautiful scenery, is also the most interesting. For the adventurous traveler interested in archaeology and geology, Middle Caicos is a veritable untrodden paradise. Along the northern coast, towering limestone cliffs drop sharply to placid, white secluded beaches. These bluffs offer a dramatic panorama seldom experienced on other subtropical islands.

Conch Bar is the largest of three settlements and the location of the island's only telephone, guest house, and airplane runway. Nearby are the barely explored, cathedral-size caves where Lucayan Indian artifacts have recently been discovered. The caves are impressive: pure white stalactites and stalagmites and mysterious underground salt lakes. Several of the entrances to the different caves are slightly hidden by large calcite pillars, while some are underwater. However, once the entrances are located, there is no difficulty finding the various chambers.

Between the villages of Bambarra and Lorimer are the interesting ruins of a settlement of the Arawak and Lucayan Indians. Two miles south is Big Pond, a rich and varied plant and animal life nature reserve.

At Douglas Taylor's four-room guest house in Conch Bar Settlement, visitors are greeted by some of the most hospitable inhabitants of these islands. Douglas Taylor can arrange island excursions or bonefishing or point you in the right direction for excellent beachcombing and shelling among the secluded hideaways on the northern coast.

WHERE TO STAY

Douglas Taylor's Guest House
Conch Bar Settlement
Middle Caicos
Turks and Caicos, British West Indies
Telephone: (809) 946-3322

RESTAURANTS

The only food on Middle Caicos is served at your hotel or guest house.

HOW TO GET THERE

There are daily 35-minute flights from Providenciales to Middle Caicos on Turks and Caicos National Air.

South Caicos

South Caicos Island has long been an important export-oriented fishing center. Along the west coast, the shallow water of the Caicos Bank is the home of the most important single industry—the harvesting and export of conch and spiny lobster. The Island's four blast-freeze plants process over 750,000 pounds of lobster for export annually.

But South Caicos is far from spoiled by its industry. The southern coast offers outstanding diving and beautiful beaches of white sand. There is easy access to fine diving along the drop-off with wall diving only minutes from shore. The scuba diver will delight in the multitude and variety of marine life. Loggerhead turtles, barracudas, spotted eagle rays, octopuses, grouper, and snapper abound. This area is also well known for the huge wall-growing sponges that reach lengths of 100 to 150 feet.

Cockburn Harbour, the main settlement, is the best natural harbor in the Caicos Islands and provides good protection for yachts in almost any weather. Here you will find grocery stores, a clinic, a telephone station, and overnight accommodations. A good view of Cockburn Harbour can be enjoyed from Highlands, a nineteenth-century house.

WHERE TO STAY

Club Carib Harbour Hotel
Cockburn Harbour
South Caicos
Turks and Caicos, British West Indies
Telephone: (800) 328-2288
This two-story hotel with veranda also has eight two-room suites one mile away at the Flamingo Resort, owned by Club Carib. Rates are $50 for two.

RESTAURANTS

The only food on South Caicos is served at your guest house or hotel.

HOW TO GET THERE

There are daily 20-minute flights from Providenciales to South Caicos on Turks and Caicos National Air.

Salt Cay

Just five minutes by air from Grand Turk, Salt Cay is a peaceful, quiet, and colorful island with a magnificent beach bordering the north coast. The windmills that once powered the salt industry add an exotic touch to the landscape, and nineteenth-century architecture slowly turns to ruins in the warm Salt Cay sun.

WHERE TO STAY

American House
Salt Cay
Turks and Caicos, British West Indies
The American House was constructed in 1839 and has recently been refurbished. Rooms are large and airy, many with verandas built in the Bermuda style. The ocean is only twenty-five feet from the back door! Rates: $60 per room.

Mount Pleasant Guest House
Salt Cay
Turks and Caicos, British West Indies
Telephone: (809) 946-6927

Simple accommodations and renowned native dishes are featured at this five-room guest house, a friendly home away from home.

The Windmills at Salt Cay
Salt Cay
Turks and Caicos, British West Indies
Telephone: (809) 946-6962
Patricia and Guy Lovelace provide a warm welcome to their small and comfortable windmills, where cottages and suites face a two-mile stretch of beach. The daily rate starts at $275 per couple in low season ($450 in winter) but include everything, even the wine at dinner.

RESTAURANTS

On Salt Cay, the only food available is served at your guest house or hotel.

HOW TO GET THERE

There are flights Monday, Wednesday, and Friday on Turks and Caicos National Air from Grand Turk. Flying time is five minutes. Hotels also arrange boat transportation.

Grand Turk

Divers are often the first visitors to discover an un-spoiled island. That certainly is the case with Grand Turk, a six-mile-long British colony with a flat, sandy coastline and nineteenth-century capital at Cockburn Town. Flying in on an eight-passenger TAC National plane, I could see the dive boats parked along the island's reef.

While the divers had obviously come for the island's offshore attractions, this was also an island to enjoy by foot or bike. The buildings facing the sea along Front Street were in a charming weathered state, reflecting their age and endurance. On a narrow side street, horses grazed on the dry lawn of an abandoned house. This sleepy, endearing town had just enough amenities for comfort without spoiling its nineteenth-century colonial past. Tiny restaurants, some with just one table, occupied the boat houses along the sea.

The salt mines started by settlers from Bermuda once brought wealth and prosperity to Grand Turk, inspiring the construction of a number of fine buildings and churches: Waterloo House (1815), now the governor's residence; a Victorian library; and an attractive wood and limestone

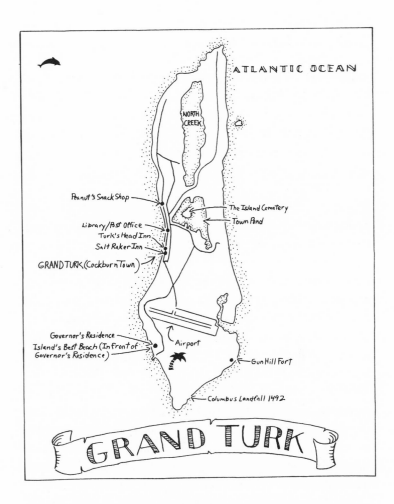

Government House, which is still the colony's administrative center.

Facing the beach near town, the 180-year-old main house of Salt Raker Inn looked inviting. Once I saw the rear garden and attractive open-air dining area, I knew I would be settling in for a while.

The gracious hospitality of the new owners more than compensated for the inn's slight feeling of disrepair. They were fresh from England with enthusiastic plans to overcome the inn's deferred maintenance. Martin unlocked one of the garden sheds and presented me with a bicycle. I was off in a flash to explore this quiet, friendly island.

NOTEWORTHY

Swimming: Governor's Beach, only a ten-minute bicycle ride from town, offers excellent swimming and snorkeling.

Scuba: The diving on Grand Turk is superb. The 6,000-foot-deep underwater "Grand Canyon" of coral is one of the natural wonders of the world. The diving instructors at Turks Island Divers Ltd. (Kittina Hotel, Box 42, Grand Turk, Turks and Caicos, BWI; [809] 946-2386) are excellent and will point out incredible marine creatures, purple tube sponges, and black coral.

Bird-watching: Gibb and Round Cay Bird Sanctuaries are home to many interesting species.

Music: Ask around town for ripsaw music. You may be lucky and get a chance to hear Joe Robinson and his Grand Turk High School Dancers, led by Terry Robinson. Music on Grand Turk is informal and noncommercial.

Camping: No public camping facilities are provided in the islands; however, camping is permitted. It is recommended that you contact local police or the island magistrate, stating your intentions and the proposed location of your campsite.

Good Buys: For under a dollar, one can buy a handful of fascinating Turks and Caicos stamps. My purchase of a series of eighteenth-century boats will make a fine gift, either framed or laminated as a bookmark. The post office is easy to find on Front Street, next to the government offices.

WHERE TO STAY

Columbus House
Box 97
Grand Turk
Turks and Caicos, British West Indies
Telephone: (809) 946-2517
The Columbus, named after the discoverer of the New World (whose landfall is believed by some to be at Grand Turk, and not at San Salvador as commonly held), is a quaint, two-story roadside inn, 150 feet from the main beach. Rates: $35 single, $50 double, with discounts for longer-term guests. Dive packages also available.

Turks Head Inn
P.O. Box 58
Grand Turk
Turks and Caicos, British West Indies
Telephone: (809) 946-2466
Located in an old garden with towering trees, this romantic 100-year-old inn has a split-level covered veranda and four-poster beds. Adjacent to the inn are the Driftwood Cottages, which rent for $75 per night. Rooms in the main lodge, facing the sea, range from $45 for a single to $70 for a double.

Salt Raker Inn

Box 1
Grand Turk
Turks and Caicos, British West Indies
Telephone: (809) 946-2260
The informal 180-year-old main house is of Bermudian architecture and includes three large, airy suites overlooking the sea at Salt Raker's own beach. In the lodge you will find a well-stocked library, maps, and travel information. In the back, several basic cottages are scattered throughout the garden. The manager-owner is very warm and helpful. Rates start at $50 single, $65 double.

Hotel Kittina

Grand Turk
Turks and Caicos, British West Indies
Telephone: (809) 946-2232
Just a few feet from the beach, the Kittina has forty-three clean, modern rooms and is the largest hotel on the island. Rooms in the two-story structure face the sea or a courtyard. Rates start at $65 single, $85 double; an oceanfront suite is $140.

RESTAURANTS

Directly on the beach at the north of Front Street, Peanuts Snak Shop has but one table and a few benches. The friendly owner, Peanuts Butterfield, cooks delicious conch fritters on her little outdoor gas burner. Ask to see her family photo album.

Turks Head. A thatched roof shelters diners at this century-old establishment that serves consistently good food, especially the fish dishes.

FROM MY JOURNAL

It seemed fitting that I would leave this friendly island with the only plates of the next issue of the *Conch News*. The paper's new owner-editor had entrusted me, a virtual stranger, with their safe delivery to the printer in Miami. The airport waiting room could hardly be called crowded: only six of us were flying out that day to Providenciales and Miami. My fellow passengers—the governor, his wife, and male secretary-bodyguard—fit their English role as perfectly as E. M. Forster characters. As they sat beside me on the eight-passenger plane, I thought what a pleasant and relaxed assignment they must have: not too much work, a fine colonial house to call home, and the island's best beach only steps away.

HOW TO GET THERE

There is nonstop service to Grand Turk from Miami on Pan American World Airways.

PRACTICAL TIPS

Immigration: U.S. citizens need some proof of citizenship such as a voter's registration card, birth certificate, or passport. All visitors must have an ongoing or return ticket. Departure tax is $10.

Currency: The unit of currency is U.S. dollars.

Health: Avoid tap water on Grand Turk, Salt Cay, and South Caicos.

PUERTO RICO'S ISLANDS

Over the past decade, a few selective travelers have discovered the secluded delights of two relatively unknown Puerto Rican islands, Vieques and Culebra. Visited by Columbus on his second New World voyage in 1493 and once known as the Spanish Virgin Islands, these two small islands are only a few miles off the east coast of Puerto Rico, but they remain essentially undiscovered by tourists. Throughout most of the twentieth century, they have been under the jurisdiction of the United States. From 1901, Culebra was the site of a naval reservation, and from World War II through the mid-1970s, the island was used for U.S. Navy gunnery and bombing practice. There is no longer a military presence on Culebra. In 1948, the navy took possession of two-thirds of the land on Vieques, and while both the navy and marines maintain training bases on the island, much of the land has been leased for cattle grazing. The sailors and marines seem to have a minimal impact on life on Vieques, although their presence is still an object of native protest. The populations of both Culebra and Vieques have grown in the past decade, after a precipitous decline caused by military maneuvers. Now, the two islands are characterized by an easygoing social atmosphere to complement the splendid weather, beautiful geography, and relaxing pace.

Vieques

Driving from the tiny airport on the north coast of Vieques through the four miles of rolling hills to Esperanza, located on the south side of the island where most vacationers stay, the unique appeal of this Puerto Rican island begins to reveal itself. Cattle graze contentedly on the scrubby hillsides, accompanied by the lanky, white African egrets that keep them free of insects. Arching expanses of white beach flash into view through lush foliage. Sunlight filters through palm, mango, and flamboyant trees, dappling the roadway with dazzling patterns of shadow and light. A mere six miles from the east end of Puerto Rico, Vieques is light years removed from the frantic pace of modern civilization. This 51-square-mile island (21 miles long and 1 to 5 miles wide) boasts some of the most beautiful beaches in the Caribbean and a way of life that harkens back to another century.

Once the home of 25,000 Spanish-speaking people, Vieques was a major sugar-producing island. None of the four sugar mills remains today, however, and the population is down to about 8,000, most of whom depend on cattle farming, fishing, and light industry for their livelihood and live in the central section of the island, between the eastern and western U.S. military reserves. The chief town is Isabel Segunda on the northern side, with about 3,500 residents. But most visitors stay near Esperanza, a strip of beach on the southern coast. Vieques was used as a location for the films *Lord of the Flies* and *Heartbreak Ridge*, but the island is noted far more for its magnificent beaches and abundant wildlife, including birds, lizards, crabs, mongooses, and wild *paso fino* (fine-gait) horses. The temperature seldom varies much from 80 degrees F year-round, with refreshing breezes blowing in from the sea and rainfall averaging only 47 inches per year. Diving, snorkeling, and nighttime trips to the spectacular Phosphorescent Bay are available through Vieques Divers in Esperanza.

Getting around the island is remarkably easy, whether or not you rent a jeep, car, motor scooter, or bicycle. The public vans, "publicos," will pick you up and drop you off

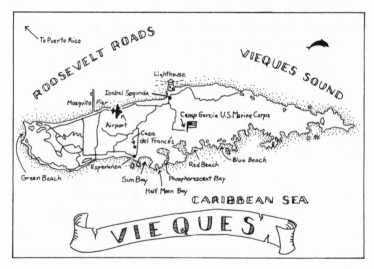

anywhere on their route for one dollar, and for a negotiated fee they will become taxis, taking you wherever you like. Once you are in Esperanza or Isabel Segunda, everything is within walking distance.

One of our favorite walks was from Sun Bay, near Esperanza, to Media Luna and Navia. For much of the morning, we were the only swimmers on the vast expanse of beach at Sun Bay. Walking along the road that winds around to Media Luna, we encountered mongooses and several of the island's small wild horses. Although there were signs of previous visitors to this sheltered bay, once again we were alone on the beach. Continuing on to Navia, we finally encountered a "crowd," about six other people on the long strip of white sand. We spent the rest of the afternoon watching the sand crabs dart in and out of their holes and napping in the softening afternoon sunshine, lulled by the sounds of the breeze and surf.

The island of Vieques is not all that remote—being so easily accessible from Puerto Rico—but with its many secluded beaches, scattered population, and light tourist trade, it has all the advantages of being off the beaten track.

NOTEWORTHY

You could spend weeks just exploring the many beaches of Vieques, and all are worth investigating.

Sun Bay is a mile-and-a-half-long, crescent-shaped beach in a public park just east of Esperanza. Coconut palms line the shore, providing ample shade. The one- to two-foot waves are just high enough to make swimming interesting. The government maintains the beach, parking lot, picnic tables, and bathhouse, but a "crowd" might amount to a dozen people on the entire beach. Admission is $1 per car.

Media Luna ("Half Moon") is a small, enclosed beach farther to the east from Sun Bay. Here you can wade out 100 yards or more in warm, absolutely still water.

Navia (also called "Third Beach") is beyond Media Luna and is one of the most beautiful on the island. Waves roll in from the ocean past a rocky promontory, and sand crabs dash in and out of their holes in the beach.

Green Beach, at the western end of Vieques, is acces-

sible, with a day pass, through the naval reservation. It is long, empty, and gorgeous, affording a fine view back to Puerto Rico.

Isabel Segunda, the main population center of Vieques, was founded in 1843 and is worth a morning or afternoon of exploration. A deserted lighthouse, built in 1896, rises sixty-eight feet above the harbor. High on the hill behind town, El Fortin, a partially restored 145-year-old Spanish fort (the last one constructed in New World), allows a grand view of the city and the northern coastline.

WHERE TO STAY

Casa Del Francés
P.O. Box 458
Vieques, Puerto Rico 00765
Telephone: (809) 741-3751
Irving Greenblatt, a cantankerous retired businessman from Boston, runs what many people consider to be "the only place to stay" on Vieques. His hotel is a revamped turn-of-the-century French sugar plantation, sitting on a hill above Esperanza. The downstairs rooms have seventeen-foot ceilings and open out onto sunny verandas. Not all rooms are equally spacious or ideally located. Meals are served in a classically "tropical," partially open dining room overlooking the cloistered swimming pool, and evening socializing revolves around a charming outdoor bar, surrounded by the lush garden foliage. Irving is one of the island's most notable characters, and his staff takes good care of the Casa guests, many of whom return year after year. But the marvelous old building itself is showing distressing signs of disrepair and will soon need the kind of serious attention that Irving puts into creating atmosphere.

Rates in the summer season, April 30 to December 1,

are $55; in the winter, December 1 to April 30, $79. Note: $20 per person is automatically added for continental breakfast and dinner.

Posada Vista Mar
P.O. Box 495
Vieques, Puerto Rico 00765
Telephone: (809) 741-8716 or 8719
The best bargain, the most gracious hospitality, and the best native cooking are available at this humble guest house on a low hill beyond the west end of Esperanza. An unbelievably thoughtful native Vieques woman named Olga rents out a half dozen small, clean, but spartan rooms behind her screened-in restaurant. The sounds of crickets and the island's famous tree frogs (*coqi*) create a vibrant chorus at night, and the bleating of Olga's goats combines with the crowing of roosters in the early morning. Rates are $25 single or double. Olga also has an apartment available for longer rentals.

The Trade Winds
P.O. Box 1012
Vieques, Puerto Rico 00765
Telephone: (809) 741-8666 or 8368
Located on the strip at Esperanza, this well-maintained guest house provides fairly modern accommodations right across the road from the beach. Rates start at $35.50 single and $45.50 double.

Villa Esperanza
Calle Flamboyan, Esperanza
Vieques, Puerto Rico 00765
Telephone: (809) 741-8588
This ambitious parador, situated on the site of an old sugar plantation at the east end of Esperanza, has modern villa apartments in configurations that can be rented as one- or two-bedroom units. The closest thing to a resort on Vieques, Villa Esperanza features a restaurant, tennis courts, scooter and jeep rentals, and private beach access. Rates are $90 double.

RESTAURANTS

Posada Vista Mar offers superb and inexpensive native cuisine, specializing in fried whole fish—grouper or snapper —served with rice and *arepas* (sweet or savory fried dough).

El Quenepo, across the street from the beach at Esperanza, is operated by the garrulous Mario, a former Brooklyn resident, who returned to Vieques and now prepares all varieties of seafood—crab, fish, lobster, octopus, conch— specializing in soups and salads as well as entrées. For lunch, a meal of black beans, rice, and arepas is perfect.

Bananas is the "hot spot" at Esperanza, attracting what young tourist crowd there is to its outdoor bar facing the beach. It is especially popular with those who want a taste of such American standards as burgers, chili, and pizza, and it offers the most active nightlife on the weekends. Bananas also has several very basic rooms for rent in back.

The Trade Winds boasts the best ocean view from its attractive restaurant and bar to go along with its popular lunch and dinner menus of creative meat and seafood dishes.

FROM MY JOURNAL

The goats are grazing outside our window at the Posada Vista Mar. Cocks are crowing throughout the neighborhood, helping us rise before dawn so we can catch the morning ferry to Fajardo. Olga taps gently at our door to make sure we're awake. In her little screened-in restaurant, she serves us coffee "on the house" and tells us what she knows about the neighboring island, Culebra. She says good-bye with a kiss on the cheek and a sincere wish that we will return someday.

HOW TO GET THERE

Crownair flies ten-seat planes to Vieques from San Juan's Isla Verde International Airport, and other airlines such as Air Link and Flamenco fly in from Isla Grande Airport. A 400-passenger ferry leaves Fajardo, on the east end of Puerto Rico, twice daily and arrives at the terminal in Isabel Segunda. Publico service is available from both the Vieques airport and Isabel Segunda to your destination on Vieques.

Culebra

At El Mini-Mas market in central Dewey, Winnie and Virginia stand behind the counter and generously share stories and information about their island. They warn that in February and March the hotels and guest houses are "booked solid" (with about 100 vacationers). They recommend returning in April to watch thousands of sooty terns build their nests on the island's rocky ledges. They explain that the strange garden down the street—the one full of ceramic animals, painted truck tires, sea shells, and tortoise shells arranged into novel sculptures—belongs to "Cato," Winnie's aunt. They express their pleasure at the fact that few tourists come over from Puerto Rico, thus leaving their island to bask in its tranquil isolation. The unforced friendliness of Winnie and Virginia and the undisturbed natural wonders of Culebra which they describe are at the heart of this charming, unspoiled island's appeal.

On Puerto Rico and even on nearby Vieques, most people tell you that there is "nothing to do" on Culebra. They could not be further off the mark. A national wildlife refuge, mangrove forests, spectacular beaches, a sheltered deep-water bay, and extensive coral reefs are among the

scenic attractions complemented by the warm hospitality of the nearly 2,000, mostly English-speaking, residents. The eleven-square-mile island, located nineteen miles east of Puerto Rico, is the largest of twenty-four islands and cays that make up a small-scale archipelago. Culebra is teeming with wildlife, including sea turtles, giant lizards, and more than eighty-five species of birds, and its rolling hills, rising to gentle 300-foot peaks, invite exploration on foot or bicycle.

The human population, mostly descended from Spanish settlers, is centered in the small, sleepy town of Dewey (known locally as "Puebla"), located on beautiful Ensenada Honda ("deep bay"). About 300 Culebrans work at the pharmaceutical equipment manufacturing company in Dewey, and most others, including several dozen transplanted North Americans and Europeans, are self-employed in services or fishing. Full employment and social harmony keep the island crime-free and wonderfully relaxed. Although the architecture of Dewey is unremarkable, barely reflecting the island's Spanish origins, the town is nonetheless attractive, with an impressive government building, interesting churches, a charming post office, an irresistible bakery, and pastel-colored houses packed close together on narrow streets. Culebra would seem ripe for development, and the number of cars and trucks on the roads is indeed surprising. But the island's reliance on rainwater, gathered in rooftop cisterns, and the preservation of lands in the National Refuge restrict the rate and scope of growth. Private homes for vacationers and retirees continue to be built outside Dewey, but large-scale tourist development seems unlikely. One of the small pleasures on

Culebra is to look up and see the airplanes carrying tourists from San Juan to St. Thomas, only fourteen miles away, and know that most of the passengers will not even notice the undiscovered island below.

NOTEWORTHY

Playa Flamenco, on the north coast, is the most spectacular of Culebra's many fine beaches. The surf can be rough, but it does not inhibit swimming, and you are likely to find yourself the sole visitor on nearly a mile of clean, white sand.

Culebrita (like Cayo Luis Peña) is a large cay that is part

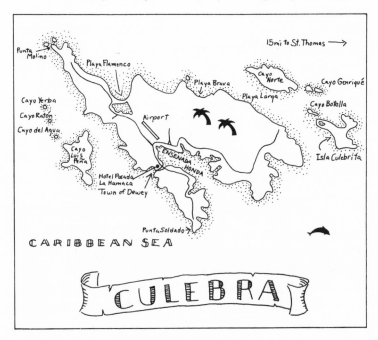

of the wildlife refuge and is home to the endangered hawksbill turtle. The nearby mile-long coral formation is one of the finest diving and snorkeling spots in the region. Culebra's offshore cays can be reached by hiring a local fishing boat or sailboat.

Mount Resaca is a large unit of the refuge land on the northern side of Culebra. It is marked by sections of dry subtropical forest, with fascinating vegetation including thorn thickets, palms, and cactus. The huge boulder formations support beautiful varieties of orchids, bromeliads, and peperomia.

Johanna's Fantasy Island, tucked away in a remote mangrove swamp, is the dream hideaway of Johanna Taylor, who built her own home in the exotic tangle of mangrove roots. A hired boat can carry you up to her dock, and if she is home, Johanna comes out and offers 25-cent tours and shows the jewelry and souvenirs that she crafts by hand.

WHERE TO STAY

Posada La Hamaca
P.O. Box 388
Culebra, Puerto Rico 00645-0388
Telephone: (809) 742-3516
The neat and clean but somewhat stark accommodations include six hotel rooms upstairs and three efficiency units downstairs, each with its own bath. Located in Dewey on the canal leading to Ensenada Honda, the hotel features an "honor bar" and barbecue on the canal-side patio and van

transportation to Flamenco Beach. Rates start at $40 double (plus a 6% hotel tax).

Club Seabourne
Fulladosa Road
Culebra, Puerto Rico 00645
Telephone: (809) 742-3169 and 742-3176
About a mile or so outside Dewey, the Seabourne is situated on a hillside with a fine view of Ensenada Honda. A spectacular flower garden slopes up to the swimming pool, screened outdoor dining room, and patio bar. The Seabourne offers rooms starting at $75 night, double; air-conditioned rooms and cottages at $95 per night per couple.

Coral Island Guest House
Box 396
Culebra, Puerto Rico 00645
Telephone: (809) 742-3266, (617) 545-5120
Located across the street from the ferry terminal, this simple hotel offers rooms for $35 daily, and complete apartments, with kitchens, for $125. Some rooms have balconies overlooking the harbor and the town, but this is a very basic spot, probably best for people who will spend most of their time enjoying such water sports as windsurfing, diving, and snorkeling. Bike rentals are $10 per day.

Weekly Rentals
A wide variety of fully furnished apartments, cottages, and houses are available for short- and long-term rentals. Full information can be provided by the Tourism Office, Box 56, Culebra, Puerto Rico 00645. Telephone: (809) 742-3521 or 742-3116.

Cielo y Mar Guest House and Culebra Island Condos
Box 207
Culebra, Puerto Rico 00645
Telephone: (809) 742-3167
For Culebra Island Condos: (201) 458-5591
Located out of town at Punta Aloe, overlooking Ensenada Honda, these are modern, fully equipped houses and apartments, with a vast array of amenities, appliances, and conveniences. They start at $350 off-season for one or three people and go up to $775 per week in peak season for four to six people.

RESTAURANTS

El Pescador, in downtown Dewey, serves delicious island food, including shark *empanadas*, pimento rellenos, lobster soup, *pastilillios, arepas,* and flan as well as steaks, chops, and pasta dishes. Louisa, the Brooklyn-born waitress, has lived in Culebra for fifteen years and can share stories in her free moments.

Marta's Island Deli, in downtown Dewey close to the ferry landing, offers a variety of local seafood, served either indoors, near the bar, or in an enclosed garden patio.

El Batay, located on the road leading out of town toward the airport, is a stark bar/pool room that serves delicious, inexpensive grilled sandwiches on locally baked bread.

Club Seabourne boasts the most elegant and most expensive ($15 to $20 range) dining on Culebra, with seafood and continental dishes prepared by a French cook and served in an attractive dining area overlooking beautiful Ensenada Honda.

FROM MY JOURNAL

The walk from Dewey to Punta Soldado winds past small houses and expansive estates along Ensenada Honda. Long brown pods hang from the trees along the road, and the seeds inside rustle in the wind like a child's rattle. The hills sloping down into the smaller bays cast great curving shadows as the sun lowers itself toward the horizon. The flowers in the Club Seabourne's immense garden are all in bloom—a rainbow of color as vibrant as the changing hues of the cloud-streaked sky at dusk. The walk to the point is long, but the views are wonderful.

HOW TO GET THERE

From the Puerto Rico mainland, daily ferry service is provided from Fajardo (on the eastern end of the island, a long drive from San Juan). The fare for the two-hour trip is about $2.50.

Flamenco Airways flies out of the Isla Grande Airport in San Juan (20 minutes from the International Airport). The thirty-minute flight costs about $23. There is also less frequent air service from St. Thomas and Vieques.

PRACTICAL TIPS

Immigration: Vieques and Culebra are part of the Puerto Rican Commonwealth of the United States, so U.S. citizens need not clear customs or immigration when traveling to or from Puerto Rico. (However, there is still an agricultural inspection on departure.)

Currency: The U.S. dollar is official currency on Culebra and Vieques.

Language: Spanish is the official language, but almost everyone speaks English.

LEEWARD ISLANDS

Saba

If all you ever did on Saba was fly in and land and then take off again, you would have experienced one of the most exhilarating adventures in the Caribbean. Imagine an airstrip that looks like a small stretch of sidewalk. Place it at the tip of a green volcanic island that rises suddenly and dramatically out of the deep blue sea. At either end of the runway, rocky cliffs drop off precipitously to the water 130 feet below. And at one end, the edge of the strip abuts the mountainside. "Of course, we're going to approach from the end that juts out over the water," you think, as your tiny, twin-engine, ten-seat STOL (Short Take-Off and Landing) airplane circles out over the ocean. Then your pilot swings the plane around and your heart jumps into your throat. The plane is aimed directly at the side of the mountain! Your breath stops short and your knuckles turn white. The plane makes a quick bank to the left, and before you know it, there's the runway. "We can't land at that angle!" the voice in your head cries. But before you can gasp again, the plane has touched down and stopped, using less than half of the 1,300-foot airstrip.

After landing on one of the shortest runways in the

world, you might think that little else on this tiny chunk of Netherlands Antilles could measure up for excitement. But remarkably, what lies in store on this five-square-mile Dutch island is all uphill. When you clear customs in the picturesque cottagelike airport, Saban taxi vans are waiting to take you from Flat Point (indeed, virtually the only flat point on Saba) up the steep road through nineteen serpentine curves, through Hell's Gate, to your destination in the equally accurately named Windwardside or over the mountain to The Bottom. Your driver will probably tell you how the road was hand-built, without any machinery, over the course of twenty years, from 1940 to 1960; that prior to that time, all goods were carried from one side of the island to the other over a grueling series of steps; and that only recently have the stone walls and eroded sections of concrete begun to be rebuilt.

As the drive continues, you might have to pinch yourself to make sure that you are not dreaming up this fairy-tale island. The buildings, painted pristine white with glossy green trim and brick-red roofs, look like they have been preserved and transplanted from some remote European Alpine village. The flowers hanging over the wall along the road create an eye-catching riot of color against the unbroken background of rich green foliage. And the views forward, up the mountain where misty clouds brush across the ridges, and back, down the steep slopes and canyons to the sea, leave you as breathless as did your landing.

Before you have reached either of Saba's two main villages, Windwardside or The Bottom, your driver will have shared a wealth of information. Helpful tips and personal stories flow freely from most of the 1,000 black and white residents of Saba, one of the friendliest islands in the Caribbean. For instance, there is Carmen, who works as waitress and bartender at Scout's Place by night, drives her own taxi van during the day, and is building a new house on the hillside overlooking The Bottom. A native of Saba, she can relate a book full of family and local history. At the Around the Bend clothing shop in Windwardside, Frida Johnson told us how her father was the first Saban to drive a jeep, and she remembers the big event when a woman first drove

on the island. What you do not learn during your first few hours on Saba, you can glean from *Saba: The First Guidebook*, an indispensable, thorough, and chatty self-published booklet by Natalie and Paul Pfanstiehl (11 Annandale Road, Newport, RI 02840).

As you soon learn, Saba is known as ''The Unspoiled Queen.'' Tourists have yet to discover this ''green gumdrop'' in significant numbers. The island's history, however, is marked by repeated discoveries and battles for sovereignty—between the Dutch, English, and French—with the Dutch taking final hold in 1816. Today, Dutch is the official language, but everyone speaks English. The Sabans, mostly descended from the original settlers and African slaves, take great pride in their island, keeping it strikingly clean and tidy. But they take great joy in sharing it as well.

What is there to do on a Caribbean island that rises so abruptly out of the sea that it has no beaches? The first thing is to explore the villages. Windwardside, on the ridge between Booby Hill and Mount Scenery, gives new depth to the adjective ''charming.'' Stroll down narrow streets past the old churches and the graveyard, and wander through the handful of shops and stores: the Superette, the Island Craft Shop, and Big Rock Market. Browse through an eye-popping selection of colorful stamps at the post office (there are even more at the main post office in The Bottom). Pick up maps, postcards, and information at the tourist office. At night, the activity is concentrated at the Chinese restaurant, at Guido's, where dancing takes precedence on the weekends, and at Cousin's Bar. But the streets are quiet and you are serenaded to sleep by crickets, frogs, and the wind rustling through broad palm leaves.

It takes about an hour to walk from Windwardside down through St. John's and Crispeen to The Bottom, but if you wave for a ride, someone is sure to pick you up. (The taxi ride costs about $5.) In addition to several quaintly officious administrative buildings in The Bottom, you will find the Saba Artisan Foundation, selling the island's famous lacelike drawn needlework, T-shirts, and several varieties of Saba Spice, a sweet and potent homemade concoction of mulled 151-proof rum; Earl's Snack Bar, Saba's answer to fast food; the splendid little Corner View Bakery, selling breads, tarts, and johnnycake; Nicholson's Supermarket; and the best native cooking on the island at Queenie's Serving Spoon.

After exploring Saba's "civilization," try the walks to Fort Bay or Ladder Bay from The Bottom; up Booby Hill or to the Lookout from Windwardside; a botanical tour with Anna Keene; or up the challenging 1,064 steps of Mt. Scenery to an elevation of nearly 3,000 feet. When you are ready for a swim, the lack of beaches is no obstacle. You can swim and snorkel off the pier at Fort Bay. If you scuba dive, you will quickly learn that Saba is one of the great unspoiled diving locales of the eastern Caribbean. Two diving facilities—Edward Arnold's Saba Deep and Joan and Lou Bourque's Sea Saba—will assist you in exploring Saba's recently established Marine Park. Underwater visibility averages seventy-five to 125 feet, and at the two dozen or so dive spots you will find towering walls and pinnacles, giant coral mounds, sea fans, sponges, dense schools of fish, and scores of crustaceans.

During our first afternoon and evening on Saba, we

began to feel at home. After another day, we had caught on to the Saban courtesy of waving to everyone you meet on the road, and we made friends with Tipsy, the one-and-a-half-eared cat who jumps into your lap at Scout's Place. By the third day, we knew how hard it was going to be to leave this mountainous emerald paradise, and how easy it would be to return.

NOTEWORTHY

The hike up Mt. Scenery, via the 1,064 stone steps, is steep and arduous at times. Most hikers average about an hour and twenty minutes to the top. But along the way you are rewarded with breathtaking views of all the settlements. The vegetation assumes giant proportions in the near rain forest setting. I sat for nearly an hour at the top, staring across the sea at St. Eustatius (Statia) and watching the clouds form and blow over the island as the cold sea air hit the warm air rising from the land.

The Saba Museum, located near Captain's Quarters in Windwardside, was established in honor of Harry Luke Johnson, whose dream it was to complete such a project. The memorabilia includes antique furniture, glassware, tools, and photographs and clippings relating the twentieth-century history of Saba.

WHERE TO STAY

Scout's Place
Windwardside, Saba, Netherlands Antilles
Telephone: (599) 4-62205

Scout's Place proves that paradise need not be expensive. Dianna Medero manages five rooms and a homey one-bedroom apartment. (A new wing of rooms was completed in 1987.) The gingerbread-trimmed main building commands a gorgeous view of the Caribbean, especially from the patio bar and outdoor dining room. Dianna serves the island's best breakfast (bacon, eggs, fat slices of homemade toast, juice, coffee or tea) in a cozy inside dining room off the kitchen. In the late morning, several locals and taxi drivers gather at the bar for coffee and conversation. The kitchen turns out hearty lunches and full-course dinners. Rates are $50 double, with breakfast and dinner included. (For a small extra charge, Dianna will prepare lobster on special order.)

Captain's Quarters
Windwardside, Saba, Netherlands Antilles
Telephone: (599) 4-62377; fax: (599) 4-2246
Perched on the verdant hillside below Scout's Place, Captain's Quarters is a beautifully restored former sea captain's home. Its ten rooms are neatly furnished, some with antique four-poster beds. The outdoor dining pavilion and terrace bar are vital centers of social activity, as is the swimming pool, unique among Saba's hotels. Full-course dinners feature lobster, steak, poultry, or fish, and reservations are required. The hotel closes down for the month of September for maintenance. Rates are $85 (summer) and $110 double, plus room tax and service charge, with Modified American Plan available for $30 per person. Rates include continental breakfast.

Juliana's
Windwardside, Saba, Netherlands Antilles
Telephone: (599) 4-62269
Juliana and Franklin manage a group of charming guest rooms, cottage, and apartment, each with bath, balcony, and views of the sea, gardens, and mountain scenery. Rooms are modern and immaculate, with sun deck and rec room for guests. Rates are $55 single, $75 double in winter; $50 single and $65 double in summer. Cottage, $100 winter, $80 summer. Apartment, $95 winter, $75 summer.

Cranston's Antique Inn
The Bottom, Saba, Netherlands Antilles
Telephone: (599) 4-63218 or 63203
Originally built as a government guest house for visiting officials, this restored two-story Victorian house came under private management in 1964. Mr. J. C. Cranston and his son Edward have gradually turned the old building into a charming inn. The rooms are furnished with antiques and locally handcrafted curtains and coverlets. The tropical garden bar is a favorite afternoon and evening watering spot in The Bottom, and the recently completed dining gazebos provide romantic settings for meals. Rates are $70 double, breakfast included.

House and Apartment Rentals
A variety of cottages, apartments, and houses in Hell's Gate, Windwardside, and Booby Hill are available for daily, weekly, and monthly rental, with rates ranging from $25 per day to $150 per week and $600 per month. The Saba Tourist Bureau maintains and publishes current listings. Telephone 599-4-62231.

RESTAURANTS

Queenie's Serving Spoon: "I have heart like marshmallow," Queenie Simmons told us when she was explaining the list of names on the wall. They were local Sabans who had not yet paid for meals she prepared on credit. Queenie and her daughters, Verna and Connie, also have a magic touch with the best down-home West Indian cuisine on Saba. Located on a back street of The Bottom, Queenie's gaily painted and wildly decorated little café has eight tables beneath home-made crepe paper "fly-catchers." For lunch, Queenie serves enormous portions of chicken in her special peanut butter sauce, with rice, greens, and fresh french fries. Call ahead for dinner and she will prepare curried goat, stuffed onion fish, muffin dumplings, and banana or pumpkin fritters. She makes a dark, powerful Saba Spice as well. Her full-page typed receipts include the salutation, "So my loveing friends i am now thanking you all and please come back again be looking out for you all soon." The feeling is genuine, and mutual.

The Saba Chinese Bar and Restaurant, in Windwardside, is famous for its egg rolls, but then it has little competition. This Caribbean anomaly serves from an extensive menu of Cantonese food and selected local dishes. At night, the bar often becomes crowded and raucous, and you can sometimes hear the music a block away.

Guido's, behind the post office and the library in Windwardside, serves pizza, made to order, all day. In the afternoon you can play a quiet game of darts, but at night the bar becomes a gathering spot for young Sabans and tourists, and the place jumps with dancers on the weekends.

FROM MY JOURNAL

How can an island without beaches be such a paradise?
Maybe it's precisely because it has no beaches, no surfers
slicing through the waves or body-beautiful sun worship-
pers draped all over the shoreline. The island has a real old-
world feel; the villages are permanently settled into the
mountains and the customs are settled into the people. This
is their home, above all, and they welcome visitors more as
guests in their home than as tourists in their "facilities."
Lunch at Queenie's, undisturbed snorkeling near the pier,
fresh lobster for dinner, and a breezy late-night walk under
a bright canopy of stars—what else is there?

HOW TO GET THERE

Pan Am, American, and Eastern airlines provide regular service to St. Maarten. Windward Air flies from St. Maarten to
Saba three times a day. The flights are often booked solid,
so be sure to reconfirm and check in early. The flight to
Saba takes fifteen minutes, unless a stop is added at Statia.

The speedboat *Style* makes the one-hour trip from
Phillipsburg, St. Maarten, to Saba three times a week, docking at Fort Bay.

PRACTICAL TIPS

Immigration: A valid passport, birth certificate, or alien
registration card is required for entry, plus a return or
onward transportation ticket. There is a $1 departure tax.

Currency: The official currency is the Netherlands Antilles florin (or guilder), with an exchange rate of approximately 1.77 florins to the U.S. dollar. But U.S. currency is routinely accepted throughout the island.

Language: Saba's official language is Dutch, but everyone on the island speaks English.

Barbuda

Paradise sometimes appears in the most peculiar and unexpected settings. Flying from Antigua into its sister island of Barbuda, one looks down on a rather uninviting landscape of flat, scrubby terrain. No rolling hills, winding rivers, spectacular cliffs, or waterfalls beckon the airborne traveler descending to a forsaken-looking, water-bound patch of earth. But as the small plane eases down in a graceful arc toward the small landing strip at Codrington, the pink and white rim of the island starts to reveal Barbuda's very special story. For here, effectively removed from all the commercial trappings of a conventional Caribbean vacation, along the edge of sixty-two square miles of unremarkable land, are miles and miles of magnificent, unspoiled beaches—among the most beautiful and least exploited in the Caribbean, if not the world. Barbuda is so rich in sandy beaches that a sand exportation business sends the "excess" to larger Caribbean islands for construction and restoration of their more heavily touristed beaches. And yet only a few hundred visitors venture the twenty-five miles from Antigua each year to enjoy the breathtakingly idyllic pleasures of Barbuda's unspoiled coastal rim.

Also visible from the air are dark brown and gray patches that mottle the gorgeous azure blue sea surrounding the island. These are the shadows of coral reefs—acres of coral reefs that lie unexplored in Barbuda's shallow waters. So even before landing, you have glimpsed the unique appeal of this wonderfully undiscovered island.

At the two-room Barbuda airport, a dozen or so people await the arrival of each plane. We were greeted by George (a.k.a. Profit) Burton, the proprietor of the Sunset View Resort, ready to recruit guests for his nearby hotel. Later in the morning, George loaded us into his truck and provided a tour of the island. The road was exceptionally rough, pitted with ruts and holes, but George seemed to know every inch. He pointed out a coconut plantation, the Martello Tower, the sand-loading operation. He accompanied us to Coco Point, past a sign that warned the driver to watch for low-flying aircraft. Less than a mile north of Coco Point, he pulled his truck over to a slight opening in the dense brush and dropped us off at a gorgeous stretch of beach that we had to ourselves for the rest of the day. The sand was white and soft, and the calm waters had rock and coral formations within wading distance. Small fish circled around our ankles, practically playing tag with us as we swam. Like all the hosts on Barbuda, George Burton (one of many Barbudan Burtons) is a repository of information and tips, providing gracious hospitality and service to visitors. When we told him we had spotted a lobster underneath a rock ledge in the shallow waters, he told us we were "very lucky." Indeed we were.

Barbuda is the "lesser" half of the two-island country

Antigua-Barbuda, which gained its independence from Britain in 1983. Most of its 1,300 black residents live in Codrington, a rustic village situated on the southeast side of the large Western or Codrington Lagoon. Bird-watchers will be fascinated by the great variety of species that nest on the island, especially at the Frigate Bird Sanctuary, accessible by private boat. Hunters occasionally roam through the brush inland or around the island's salt ponds in pursuit of wild boar, deer, and duck. And if it is possible to tire of the absolute natural peace of sunning, swimming, and snorkeling at any of the white sand and dazzling pink, shell-laden beaches, there are many landmarks to investigate such as the ruins of Sir William Codrington's Highland House estate, the Indian caves, or the Martello Tower, built by Spanish colonists as a beacon for ships at sea. Apparently, many seafarers did not spy the land in time, as some sixty or more ships crashed and sank in Barbuda's shallow, reef-bound waters. The wrecks provide fascinating excursions for scuba divers.

I discovered one of Barbuda's most interesting social phenomena during a walk through Codrington at dusk. As George Burton later explained, every morning the village residents open their gates and let their small herds of goats roam and graze freely around the island. Around such public buildings as the school and government house, the goats mow the wild grass into neat, closely cropped lawns. As sunset approaches, the goats migrate back to town in herds one hundred or more strong. Once they reach the streets of Codrington, they break off into smaller groups and walk confidently through the neighborhood to find their own yard. It is an enlightening and moving experience to walk through the droves of tame, bleating goats as they are instinctively returning home. Once night falls, so does the level of activity in Codrington. This is not a tourist town. There are no souvenir shops or nightclubs, no dive shops or T-shirt concessions, just an eminently free and easy lifestyle for self-sufficient travelers who want to discover the best secluded Caribbean spots for themselves.

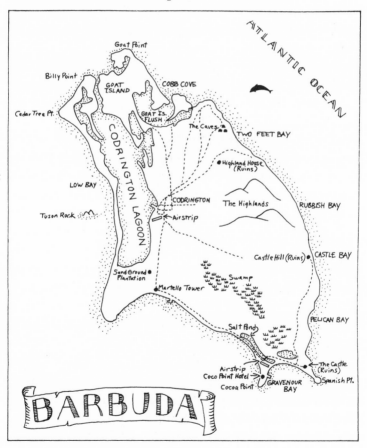

NOTEWORTHY

Stamps: If you have a few extra minutes at the Antigua airport, stop at the post office near the bank window and
browse through the beautiful Antigua-Barbuda postage
stamps. They are printed in deliciously bright colors with
pictures of fruits, flowers, and wildlife.

WHERE TO STAY

Le Village Soleil
Box 1104
St. John's, Antigua, West Indies
Telephone: (809) 460-0004
Situated on one of Barbuda's awesome south coast beaches,
this casual resort is operated by French-speaking Cana-
dians, Danie and Andre Cloutier. Their sixteen rooms are
situated in apartment and thatched-roof cottages, and they
offer fine meals and such special excursions as lobster bar-
becues on the beach. Rates are $200-$245 per day, Modified American Plan.

Sunset View Resort
Belle Village, Barbuda, West Indies
Telephone: (809) 460-0078
Located about one-quarter mile outside Codrington, near
the Lagoon, this eleven-room, two-story hotel is the most
comfortable, reasonably priced accommodation on the
island. Its simple and cozily modern rooms are neatly
appointed. The outdoor dining room and bar are especially

attractive, in a garden setting surrounded by goat-mown fields. Rates are $40 single, $60 double.

Coco Point Lodge
Box 90
St. John's, Antigua, West Indies
Telephone: (809) 462-3816
Although Barbuda would not seem a likely setting for a luxury hotel, William Cody Kelly succeeded in establishing a stunning, country clublike resort on the southern coast of the island. Single-level cottages and bungalows are situated on their own secluded sections of one of the Caribbean's most beautiful palm-lined beaches. The grounds and gardens are immaculately groomed, and the main house dining room and cocktail terrace face a breathtaking expanse of sand and sea. Vacations here are expensive barefoot escapes. The all-inclusive rates, which range from $250 to $600 per day, provide for all food, drinks, the use of tennis courts, boats, snorkeling equipment, and excursions.

GUEST HOUSES

The traveler on a more restricted budget will be able to find very basic accommodations in one of Codrington's several guest houses, including the Thomas House (which sells specially made postcards) located right next to the airport, and The Earl's, offering apartments and cottages in or near town. Detailed information is available from the Antigua-Barbuda Tourist Board in New York City: 610 5th Avenue, Suite 311, New York, NY 10020; telephone: (212) 541-4117.

RESTAURANTS

Most visitors to Barbuda eat at their hotel or guest house, but Jam City is a popular local night spot.

HOW TO GET THERE

LIAT operates regularly scheduled morning and afternoon flights from Antigua to Barbuda.

PRACTICAL TIPS

Immigration: U.S. and Canadian citizens need only proof of identity. A passport is best, but a birth certificate (an original, not a photocopy) or a voter's registration card will do. There is an $8 departure tax. A return or onward transportation ticket is required.

Currency: Barbuda uses the East Caribbean dollar (EC), with an exchange rate of approximately $2.60 EC to US$1. There is a bank at the Antigua airport where you can exchange your money before flying on to Barbuda.

Language: The official language is British English.

Montserrat

The natural beauty of Montserrat is abundantly evident as you fly in toward Blackburne Airport. The mountainous terrain is densely covered with dark green tropical foliage and forests. Misty clouds linger on the highest peaks. And the beauty only grows more intense as you get closer.

The warm hospitality of Montserrat is also abundantly evident as soon as you set foot in the tiny airport. The immigration officer asks where you are staying and offers his recommendations for lodging and car rentals, and he will register you for a temporary driver's license after you have cleared customs. (It is best, however, to make your hotel decision on your own, after considering the options.) In the next room, the customs inspector hardly looks at your luggage; he is more interested in welcoming you to Montserrat. When he asks about the nature and extent of your visit, it seems less for official reasons than out of formal courtesy. And everything is accompanied by a smile.

Magnificent natural wonders and relaxed, informal hospitality are the key attractions of Montserrat, a 39-square-mile island fifteen minutes by air from Antigua.

It is an island of wonderful contrasts. Named by Christopher Columbus when he sailed by in 1493, Montserrat was first settled by Irish colonists (with a sprinkling of Scots and English) more than 350 years ago. The Irish influence is reflected in Montserrat's appropriate title as the "Emerald Island," in such place-names as St. Patricks, Brodericks, Joe Morgan Hill, and Galway Plantation, and in the shamrock that is stamped onto your passport. But the modern population of 13,000 is mostly black and English-speaking. The island has been visited by pop music superstars because of its world-famous recording studio, yet it remains remarkably off the beaten track for most Caribbean tourists. It has a beautiful 100-acre golf course that seems anomalous amidst the vast expanses of lush unspoiled scenery. It is large enough to require auto transportation along its 115 miles of paved roads but is best explored by foot from points where the roads end.

Plymouth is the main settlement, a partially rustic, partially modern village of 3,000 located on the sheltered west coast of Montserrat. The drive from Blackburne Airport, on the east side, takes you along winding roads, through fertile farmland, past hundreds of grazing goats and cattle, up through the hills dotted with private homes, and back down to the Caribbean shore. In town, the narrow avenues are a maze of one-way streets, running past centuries-old buildings and churches and less interesting contemporary structures. Most visitors stay in or near Plymouth, taking advantage of the restaurants, car rentals, and easy access to the taxis that can carry you to the important sites north and south of town. During the day, the streets are busy, with people gathering in conversation on

the corners. But at night, the town is still and looks virtually empty, especially in the summer season, with activity
confined to the restaurants and pubs.

A hiker's paradise, with rewarding climbs and fascinating trails beckoning from all over the island, Montserrat
cannot claim to be one of the Caribbean's best beach and

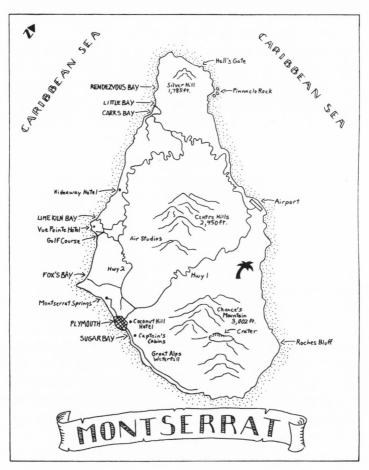

diving locales. The waters are unpredictable, the coral reefs and coves few, and many of the beaches are gray and pebbly. But the Caribbean side of the island has the gentlest and warmest water, with good snorkeling—at the best white sand beach near the Vue Pointe Hotel and at Rendezvous and Carr's Bay—and such interesting dives as The Pinnacle, off Woodlands Bay, and the Artificial Reef, where the government once dumped over 200 old cars into eighty feet of water near Fones Bay to attract sea life. Windsurfing is available at the Vue Pointe Hotel.

But here, in contrast to such beach-bound heavens as Barbuda and the Bahamas, the water is almost an adjunct to the land. The possibilities for exploring the island are virtually limitless, from the exhilarating views from Old Fort on St. George's Hill to the challenging climb up to the 3,000-foot peak of Mount Chance. Most people return to Montserrat year after year, knowing that they can feel welcomed and immediately at home yet always finding something new to discover in the island's unique geographical splendor.

NOTEWORTHY

Great Alps Waterfall: We found a shortcut that knocked at least half an hour off the hiking time to this spectacular 70-foot waterfall, but we couldn't find our junction on the way back and thus added at least another 30 minutes to the walk to our car. So it is recommended that you either hire a guide or start from the main entrance near the southern end of the island. The walk is long and humid but well worth the exertion. As you approach the falls, the ferns and

other broad-leafed plants grow to enormous heights. They add to the spiritual feeling that mounts as you finally reach the waterfall, which cascades down a sheer cliff into a small, slightly sulfurous pool. Take your time getting there and consider carrying water and a picnic lunch or snack.

Galway's Plantation: About a fifteen- or twenty-minute drive south of Plymouth and up a winding ravine, the ruins of this seventeenth-century sugar plantation are being meticulously excavated. A windmill, sugar boiling house, and great house are available for investigation. And the view that David Galway, an ambitious Irish plantation owner, commanded nearly 300 years ago has hardly changed.

Galway Soufriere is the bubbling, sulfurous center of a volcano in the southern section of Montserrat, just up the hill from Galway's plantation estate. A fascinating 20-minute walk from the road's end takes you along rugged volcanic rock to the steaming sulfur vents.

Fox's Bay Bird Sanctuary is located on the coast just north of Plymouth at Richmond Estate. Established as part of the Montserrat National Trust in 1979, it is the nesting place of egrets, herons, cuckoos, kingfishers, coots, and other species.

Stamps: Although you might start off at the Plymouth Post Office looking for stamps, be sure someone directs you to the Philatelic Building, where you could spend hours perusing the marvelous stamps at the Montserrat Stamp Shop. The natural wonders of the island, from lizards and fish to the towering peaks, are depicted in vivid color. They are among the most beautiful and sought-after stamps in the Caribbean.

The Montserrat Historical Society Museum, located in an old sugar mill near Richmond Hill, houses exhibits reflecting the natural and cultural history of the island as well as a fascinating postage stamp collection.

Air Studios: Rock stars from all over the world, including Stevie Wonder, Elton John, Paul McCartney, and Sting, have traveled to Montserrat to record at the famous Air Studios, secluded on the outskirts of Plymouth. Although they are closed to the public, you may request a tour of the sophisticated facilities by calling studio manager Yvonne Kelly for an appointment. Telephone: (809) 491-5678.

WHERE TO STAY

Vue Pointe Hotel
P.O. Box 65
Olde Towne, Montserrat, West Indies
Telephone: (809) 491-5210
The Vue Pointe has a widespread reputation as Montserrat's finest and friendliest hotel, to which many guests return year after year. But it is also the most expensive. Its twelve rooms and twenty-eight hexagonal cottages are scattered among palm trees on spacious, neatly groomed grounds. Located next to Montserrat's beautiful Belham Valley Golf Course, it has a swimming pool with a spectacular sea view and is only about 100 yards from one of the island's best beaches. The special Wednesday night barbecue with live steel band music is a popular event. Rates are $170-$205 for a double during winter with breakfast and dinner and $62-$90 summer without meals.

Montserrat Springs Hotel
P.O. Box 259
Richmond Hill, Plymouth
Montserrat, West Indies
Telephone: (809) 491-2481
There are seventeen garden rooms and six efficiency suites with kitchen at this pleasant small resort overlooking Emerald Isle Beach. Guests enjoy use of a swimming pool and two tennis courts.

Wade Inn
Parliament Street, Plymouth
Montserrat, West Indies
Telephone: (809) 491-2881
Conveniently situated in the middle of town, the Wade Inn offers very basic accommodations. Compared to the hillside and sea-view hotel, its location is rather mundane, although it makes Plymouth immediately accessible. Reasonable prices and a restaurant that is considered one of the finest in town greatly enhance its appeal. There is dancing to live music on Friday nights. Rates are $35 single and $47 double.

Apartment and Villa Rentals
Weekly and monthly rentals are available in Plymouth and its outlying areas. For information, contact the Department of Tourism, P.O. Box 7, Plymouth, Montserrat, W.I. Telephone: (809) 491-2230.

RESTAURANTS

The Pantry, in Plymouth, is a casual restaurant that is very good for home-cooked breakfast and lunch.

The Attic, upstairs in the same building as The Pantry, is popular for its homey cuisine and breezy rooftop dining with a superb view.

The Iguana, at the edge of Plymouth in Wapping, combines an informal setting with a mixed menu of unusual items such as fried Camembert, pizza, and pâtés. Student parties are sometimes rowdy, but a separate garden patio offers escape out back.

Wong Gee Cat, still sometimes called Chez Nous, is located in Plymouth, upstairs behind Ram's Market, and serves excellent West Indian and Chinese food.

The Oasis, in Plymouth, next door to the Plantation Club, is renowned for its "mountain chicken," a euphemism for giant frog legs.

FROM MY JOURNAL

We rented a car in Plymouth today and learned how to drive on the left side of the road with the steering wheel on the right—first through the narrow one-way streets of town, then on the narrow winding road to the southern end of the island. Drivers here know every curve and bump; there's no time to be nervous. Away from town, the task is easier, but it's a relief to park the car and walk off into the jungle. I'd just as soon throw the keys into the sea and stay on foot. The morning drive back over the mountain to the airport is spectacular. Mists rise from the ground dampened overnight by sudden rain showers, and the sun streams through the leftover clouds. I'm ready to toss my plane ticket into the sea as well.

HOW TO GET THERE

LIAT, British West Indies Air (BWIA), and Montserrat Air have regularly scheduled flights from Antigua to Black-burne Airport on the northeast coast of Montserrat.

PRACTICAL TIPS

Immigration: A valid passport or proof of identity is required for entry, plus a return or onward transportation ticket. The departure tax is $8.

Currency: The currency on Montserrat is the Eastern Caribbean dollar (EC), with an exchange rate of approximately $2.60 EC to US$1.

Language: It's English with a brogue, a result of the Irish legacy.

FRENCH WEST INDIES

Marie-Galante

It is an enigma that an island as large as Marie-Galante, with such superb beaches and even a unique ocean-front hotel, can be so undiscovered. Rarely will you find more than a handful of visitors. Even at Christmas, while other islands are packed to capacity, the beaches on Marie-Galante are relatively empty. The only possible explanation is that barely a word of English is spoken anywhere on the island. For the intrepid traveler who does not mind the challenge of a French-speaking island not geared to tourism, the rewards are many.

The trip from Pointe-à-Pitre, Guadeloupe, is an easy one, either by ferry (one hour) or by air (ten minutes, landing on the flat plain a few miles south of Grand-Bourg). Coming immediately into view are the sugarcane fields and idle nineteenth-century stone windmills. Grand-Bourg, a town of 10,000 inhabitants, is a busy scene of ugly concrete structures mixed with more interesting wooden buildings. The balconies over the sidewalks are similar to those in the Latin Quarter of New Orleans, and there is a covered outdoor market where colorfully dressed women sell spices, fruit, vegetables, and clothing.

To explore the island beyond the principal town of Grand-Bourg (pronounced in patois as "GAM-bo"), ten-passenger minibuses can be hailed like taxis all day from 6 a.m. to 5 p.m. You get off anywhere along the route and pay the 5F ($0.60) tariff as you exit. As you ride along the oceanfront road to the smaller towns of St. Louis and Capesterre, there is the temptation to stop as each beach becomes progressively more inviting. Snorkeling at Capesterre is excellent, and from here it is a very long swim or a short walk to les Galeries, massive and impressive rock formations that have been carved out by the surf. Continuing inland, Trou a Diable is a magnificent cave for the adventurous. It is some 550 yards long with an underground lake. Safer, perhaps, is the marvelous walk along the cliff-fringed coast with its rocky promontories and secluded coves to Caye Plate, a steep-sided crag with extensive views, where local fishermen catch crayfish of exceptional size.

Marie-Galante is a delight to explore. Each turn of the coast offers another marvelous vista, secluded cove, or immense stretch of quiet beach. Staying here is like returning to another era, before the tourism boom of the 1950s covered most islands with high-rise hotels and curio shops.

NOTEWORTHY

Habitation Murat is a baroque-style plantation manor built in the eighteenth century and destroyed by earthquake in 1843. It is now a museum with sea life exhibits. The restored windmill is the most fascinating building on the estate grounds, and from the tower there are commanding views of Dominica.

Vieux-Fort, an Old World village on a fine beach, is a fascinating collection of pile dwellings, which were common all over the island until the nineteenth century.

Plage Du Massacre is a fine, long beach with many excellent picnic spots beneath shady trees. This is a quieter, less populated part of the island.

St. Louis, a town of 4,000 inhabitants, is worth exploring on foot. The old, weathered stores and houses on the back streets are infinitely more interesting than the new

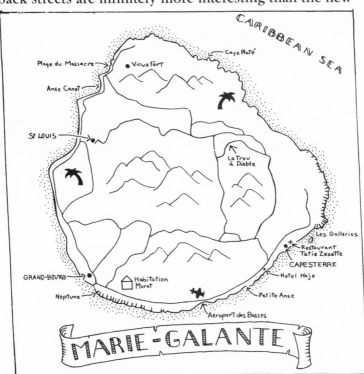

concrete of Capesterre and Grand-Bourg. Along the water-front, multicolored fishing boats glisten on the clear, calm sea in the bright sun. A fine beach is just minutes to the north by foot.

WHERE TO STAY

Hotel Hajo
Capesterre, Marie-Galante
97112 Guadeloupe, French West Indies
Telephone: (590) 97-32-76
Mediterranean in style with unusual sculpture and furniture, each of the six rooms at Hajo faces the sea. Hajo is an amazing place. Rarely will you see another guest, except at Christmas, when the total number might rise to twelve.

Food is French and Creole, excellent and hearty, served on the seaside veranda. The location could not be better: it is a ten-minute walk to village of Capesterre or a five-minute walk to one of the best beaches on the island. How Hotel Hajo can stay in operation with rates as low as $38 per day for two, offering accommodations with private bath, in a fine seaside location, is just another enigma of Marie-Galante.

Auberge de la Roche D'or
Capesterre, Marie-Galante
97122 Guadeloupe, French West Indies
Telephone: (590) 97-91-92
This is a small, basic inn, across the road from a good beach. Inexpensive.

Auberge Soledad
Grand-Bourg, Marie-Galante
97112 Guadeloupe, French West Indies
Telephone: (590) 97-75-45 or 97-74-43
Set in a garden with a sea view, this is a large house with twenty spartan rooms (eight are air conditioned). Its restaurant features Creole specialties. Rates start at $23 per couple for a standard room and $39 for an air-conditioned double.

RESTAURANTS

Tatie Zezette, Plage la Feuillere, Capesterre, offers very good Creole cuisine with vintage wine. The owner is charming, but you must speak French. Telephone: 97-96-84.

Neptune, Rue Beaurenon ze Pont, Grand-Bourg, offers delicious pizza *jambon* and reasonable French seafood dishes, including *mousseline de poisson, langoustes, coquille d'oursins gratinees, darne de daurade au poivre vert*, and wood-grilled fish and meat. Telephone: 97-96-90.

Chez Henri Et Baptiste, in Saint Louis, is a very charming, intimate restaurant with excellent food. But here, as at all restaurants on Marie-Galante, you should give them an hour's notice before you arrive so they can turn on the generator and buy the food. Since there are literally no tourists, each restaurant will be your own private dining room. No telephone.

FROM MY JOURNAL

What an adventure renting a car tonight! The owner had never seen an American driver's license and perused both sides with gleeful amazement. No deposit, no contract. Total faith and trust in this visitor from another planet. I drove off into the unexplored darkness, happy to have landed on "an island in time."

HOW TO GET THERE

There is regular ferry service (one hour, $6) from Pointe-à-Pitre, Guadeloupe to Grand-Bourg, Marie-Galante, and several daily flights on Air Guadeloupe (15 minutes, $25 one way). Reconfirm return air reservations on arrival.

Terre-de-Haut

One Caribbean island is so ideal that the visitor has to wonder why few people other than Jacques Cousteau have discovered it and made it their home. Its striking terrain, panoramic vistas, empty, breathtaking beaches and dazzling water, gracious population, fine cuisine, and refreshing paucity of tourism all conspire to make it a genuine paradise. If its dependence on rain for drinking water did not inhibit future development, I would be reluctant to even divulge the name of this, one of my very favorite islands. Fortunately, Terre-de-Haut will remain relatively unspoiled as it can sustain only a small number of visitors at any one time.

Iles des Saintes is a tiny cluster of islands seven miles off the southwestern tip of Guadeloupe. Terre-de-Haut (more often referred to as Les Saintes) is the archipelago's island metropolis, although it is less than six square miles in size with fewer than 5,000 inhabitants. And it is the only island with several choices of accommodation.

The beaches on Les Saintes are marvelous; swimming and snorkeling are excellent. But that is only one small part of this island's appeal. Because the remarkable hilly terrain

Roads
Trails

TERRE DE HAUT

of Les Saintes is unsuited for agriculture, the French never colonized the islands for anything but strategic reasons. There was no plantation system and thus no history and no legacy of slave labor. The peaceful relationship between the French and the native Santois has resulted in a minimum of racial tension and economic disparity. Poverty, unemployment, and crime are unknown here; there isn't even a jail.

Of the mere dozen vehicles on the island, most are taxi vans serving as transport to and from the airport, for school outings to the beach, or occasionally as an ambulance. The narrow concrete roads thus become extra wide "sidewalks" where you can stroll leisurely without the intrusion of motor traffic. One can walk easily anywhere on the island in less than an hour.

Terre-de-Haut is the island's major town. A picturesque little settlement of small, red-roofed houses, it is centrally located on a curving bay between the hills. These charming houses and stores are spotlessly clean and beautifully adorned with colorful vines and a myriad of flowers in dozens of pots and jars. This is not a town reconstructed for the sake of tourism; it is a neatly maintained fishing village where life revolves around the sea. Purple, pink, and mauve fishing nets are used to haul in the daily catch. What is not consumed in private homes behind eighteenth-

century doors is sold to the local restaurants. Terre-de-Haut hosts frequent weekend visitors from Guadeloupe who enjoy fine dining at the many small restaurants along the waterfront and back streets. The cuisine of Les Saintes is French and Creole and consistently superb.

NOTEWORTHY

Pain du Sucre: The tiny, exquisitely beautiful double cove at Pain du Sucre is hard to find. In fact, I only discovered it on my second visit when some locals asked the taxi van to stop on my way back to Hotel Bois Joli. Carrying towels and snorkeling gear, they disappeared suddenly on the steep path beneath the road. Their destination was this

marvelous hidden spot, where snorkeling is excellent. And, should you become thirsty or hungry, there is even a small, informal beach restaurant. To get here from town, ask the taxi van for Pain du Sucre, or take the Hotel Bois Joli boat and, for an extra few francs, ask them to stop. By foot, you can reach the cove through a hilly, forty-minute walk from town.

Pont-Pierre Beach: Totally protected by cliffs, this unspoiled, undeveloped bay is one of the most beautiful in the Caribbean. Visitors from Guadeloupe come on the weekends for the fine snorkeling and swimming, but even then it is hardly overcrowded. Limited camping is available for a nominal fee.

Fort Napoleon: Built at the beginning of the nineteenth century to replace an earlier seventeenth-century fort, Fort Napoleon contains a small museum. The thirty-minute walk is pleasant, and the views make the climb worthwhile.

Morne du Chameau: At 1,014 feet, this is the highest point on the island. From the top, you can enjoy breathtaking panoramic views of Guadeloupe to the north, Marie-Galante to the east, and Dominica to the south.

WHERE TO STAY

Hotel Bois Joli
Terre-de-Haut, Les Saintes
via Guadeloupe, French West Indies
Telephone: (590) 99-52-53
This 21-room hotel has a very private location along the

coast one mile from town. The rooms are spartan but comfortable, the choicest being those on the top floor with incredible views; the two-bedroom bungalow with kitchen and open porch is ideal for families. Swimming is excellent and the snorkeling is outstanding at the far end of the beach. You can walk or ride the taxi van into town, but the Hotel also operates a small boat into town three times daily for about $1 each way. About halfway on the very pleasant, scenic ride you will pass Jacques Cousteau's private cove. You can also rent your own boat and have more freedom and flexility. Rates at Bois Joli start at $120 for two, but this includes breakfast and dinner.

Jeanne d'Arc
Terre-de-Haut, Les Saintes
via Guadeloupe, French West Indies
Telephone: (590) 99-50-41
This small, ten-room beachfront hotel is situated at the end of the village, within walking distance of the town's plaza, wharf, and restaurants. The best rooms face the beach and rent for approximately $20 nightly per person.

Auberge des Anacardiers
La Savane, Terre-de-Haut
Les Saintes, Guadeloupe, French West Indies
Telephone: (590) 995-0990
You can be assured the warmest welcome on the island at this charming, ten-room wood chalet with swimming pool that overlooks the harbor. This is the newest addition to the island's accommodations, and the owners are trying very

hard to please their guests. Secluded and quiet, Anacardiers is just a very short walk to the town or beach. Breakfast and a superb dinner are included in the daily rate of 550 francs ($95) for two.

HOUSEKEEPING ACCOMMODATIONS

La Colline
Terre-de-Haut, Les Saintes
via Guadeloupe, French West Indies
Telephone: (590) 99-52-19
Each of these five bungalows has a small kitchen and a magnificent view of the harbor and Fort Napoleon above that. They are a three-minute walk from a beach, five minutes from town, and thirty minutes by foot from the island's best and largest beach.

Le Village Creole
Terre-de-Haut, Iles des Saintes,
Guadeloupe, French West Indies
Telephone: (590) 99-53-83
There are fully equipped kitchens and a washer at this charming one- and two-bedroom unit complex near the Hotel Kanaoa and a short walk to town. Daily rates per couple start at $120 in summer and $140 in winter.

APARTMENTS/HOUSE RENTALS

Joëlle et Jean-Claude Martin
17 bis rue Barbès
97110 Pointe-à-Pitre
Guadeloupe, French West Indies
Telephone: (590) 91-07-21

This helpful French-Canadian couple on Guadeloupe rents out an inexpensive studio and a spacious house on Terre-de-Haut. The house is ideally situated between the town (5 minutes) and the beach (10 minutes).

If you chat with the locals, you might be able to find a room in a private house, "chez l'habitant." Ask shopkeepers or consult the detailed list at the town hall.

CAMPING

Camping is allowed at Pont-Pierre Beach, one of the most beautiful undeveloped bays in the Caribbean.

RESTAURANTS

It is probably impossible to get a bad meal from any of the dozen or so small restaurants on Les Saintes. Among the local delicacies are *crabes farçis*, stuffed crab; *accra*, a small fritter of cod or malanga root; *daube de lambis*, a conch stew; *blaff*, made with fish or sea urchins; *ragoût de chartrous*, small octopus served with red beans; *poulet à la noix de coco*, local free-range chicken cooked in coconut milk. Desserts include *bananes flambé* and the Les Saintes specialty, *tourment d'amour*, coconut tarts, often sold on the streets by the island's beautiful children.

FROM MY JOURNAL

Carnival on Terre-de-Haut last night was a festival of color, music, and a small island's friendly *joie de vivre*. Young and old danced together en masse in the town plaza by the wharf. Many beautiful, painted faces were crowned with thick blond hair, Sweden's legacy to these fair islands. Next time we'll definitely want to participate with costumes.

HOW TO GET THERE

Air Guadaloupe has daily fifteen-minute flights from Pointe-à-Pitre on Guadeloupe to Terre-de-Haut. By sea, regular ferry service is offered from Trois-Rivieres on Guadeloupe (8:30 a.m. Monday through Saturday, 7:30 a.m. on Sunday). From Pointe-à-Pitre, the ferry leaves daily at 8 a.m. and returns at 4 p.m. Contact Trans-Antilles Express for schedules; telephone: (590) 83-12-45.

Terre-de-Bas

The other inhabited island of Ile des Saintes, Terre-de-Bas, is only three miles from Terre-de-Haut but is remarkably separate. Because there is no regular boat service, this small island is rarely visited. But now that overnight lodging is available, Terre-de-Bas is well worth exploring. A walker's paradise, crisscrossed with scenic hiking trails and small one-lane roads, the island can be explored at the leisurely pace found only on such undiscovered spots.

The road begins at the ferry landing at Anse des Muriers. Just a few hundred yards inland, at the first fork in the road, you encounter Arlette's Restaurant, a source of good food and valuable information about the island. The small road to the left leads to Grand Anse, a tiny village clustered around a primitive seventeenth-century church. Swimmers and snorkelers will want to take this detour to Grand Anse and enjoy refreshing drinks at the beachside "lolos."

Back on the main cross-island road past Arlette's, each bend offers a different and more spectacular view before the final descent into Petites Anses. Island life is focused here around the town hall, post office, fire station, dispensary, school, church, cemetery, hotel, and restaurant. Next to the marina, colorful "Santois" fishing boats line the beach and fishing nets dry in the warm sun.

WHERE TO STAY

Au Poisson-Volant
Petites Anses, Terre-de-Bas
Iles des Saintes
via Guadeloupe, French West Indies
Telephone: (509) 99-80-47

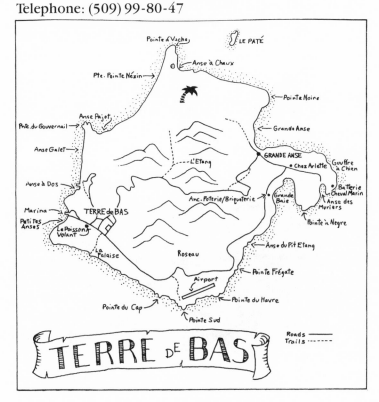

The only hotel in town has nine rooms. Rates are approximately $40 per night, per room. Delicious Creole specialties are served with advance notice.

It is possible to rent a room with meals at Chez Renaud Vala or Chez Arlette, telephone (509) 99-81-66. A knowledge of French is almost essential on Terre-de-Bas, unless you are confident that you can get by with mime and sign language.

HOW TO GET THERE

Irregular ferry service is available from Basse Terre on Guadeloupe, most likely on Monday, Wednesday, Thurs-

day, and Saturday, departing at 12:30 p.m. and arriving at Terre-de-Bas two hours later. On the boat, ask about return sailing times and days. If your French is good, you can arrange for a local fisherman to take you from Terre-de-Haut, where there is regular air and boat service, to Guadeloupe.

PRACTICAL TIPS

Since there are few hotels on Les Saintes, it is important to have a reservation in the peak seasons, December 15-March 15, Bastille Day (July 14), and Liberation Day (August 15-17).

Take a flashlight, as the roads are not lit at night, and on moonless nights the countryside beyond town is pitch dark.

Immigration: An onward or return ticket and a valid passport are required.

Currency: The French franc is the official currency and fluctuates around 6F for US$1.

Language: French is the language, but English is spoken in some hotels and restaurants.

GRENADINES

The Grenadine Islands are simply sensational. There are over 120 of them in the fifty miles between St. Vincent and Grenada, but only eleven are inhabited. They are a boat owner's paradise: very tropical, hilly islands with many fine harbors and coves, constant breezes, charming villages, friendly people, and superb, uncrowded beaches.

The most beautiful and undiscovered of the inhabited islands are now accessible to anyone willing to make the effort to get there. Several of the islands have small airports, and there is local boat service to the others.

Starting at the top in the St. Vincent Grenadines, Bequia is a well-discovered international destination. It is a beautiful island with many fine small hotels and excellent beaches. Loyal visitors return year after year to this friendly island, accessible only by boat from St. Vincent. Mustique has marvelous beaches and coves and attracts an international crowd to Cotton House and the island's fifty private houses, which give this pleasant island its celebrity status. To the south, Canouan never has more than two dozen visitors at any one time; there are just two small beachfront hotels, a handful of cars, and 600 hospitable people. Not far

away, Mayreau is a return to another century, so undiscovered that no one on Carriacou (ten miles away) knew if
there were any inhabitants or any place to spend the night!
Spectacular Union Island, with two lofty peaks rising from
the aquamarine sea, has its share of yachts but still remains
quiet and friendly. Here also are Petit St. Vincent, Palm
Island, and Young Island, the three privately owned and
fairly well-publicized resort islands of the Grenadines.

Crossing the border from the St. Vincent Grenadines
to the Grenada Grenadines, Petit Martinique and Carriacou
bring the total number to five exceptional, undiscovered
jewels in the Grenadine crown: Canouan, Mayreau, Union,
Petit Martinique, and Carriacou.

Carriacou

Carriacou's thirteen square miles of towering hill and white sand beaches make it the largest and most populated of the Grenadines. It is also one of the most beautiful and certainly the most interesting. On this rich agricultural island, the Scots settled in Windward, the French in L'Esterre, and the English in Hillsborough, leaving an influence still in evidence today. This European heritage mixes with descendants of black slaves, who have preserved many old cultural and spiritual traditions resembling the Xango of Trinidad and the voodoo cult of Haiti.

In the town of Windward, villagers of Scottish descent carry on the tradition of building wooden schooners from local white cedar. Skeletons of boats in various stages of completion are often seen on the beach, where workers use centuries-old techniques and rudimentary tools to create the West Indian trade schooner fleet. Many of the Windward boats sail in the Carriacou Regatta held during the first weekend in August. It is a wonderful time to visit, as the island's 8,000 inhabitants celebrate on land as well as sea.

The sounds of conga drums fill the air, and all eyes

turn toward the dancers, who celebrate the harvest of the land and sea with dances handed down over generations. The people of Carriacou remember the African tribes from which they came—Congo, Moko, Mandinka, Ibo, Kromanti—and their dances are sensational. The island's four-day festivities also include swimming, model boats, ball games, tug-of-war, and everyone's favorite, greasy pole.

By the Wednesday after the festival, Hillsborough town has returned to its normal level of activity. With a

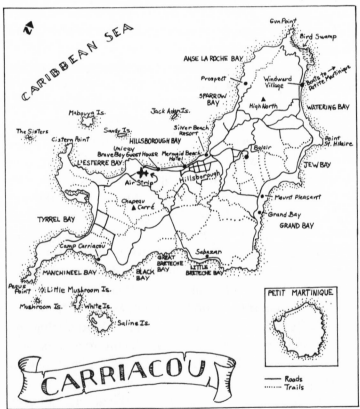

population of just under 900, there are few traffic jams, no stop lights, and no need to hurry. Main street parallels the beach. Built of stone and shingle, many of the stores have fascinating names: the Industrious Store, the Family Store (a good place to buy stamps), Morning Star Bakery, No Trust, Trust Is to Burst, and No Hell. Near the pier is the post office, the fruit and vegetable market, and the government customs office.

Leaving the town and heading north into the hills toward Windward, the nature lover will delight in the flora and fauna of this lush, tropical island. Bougainvillea and flamboyants flourish, and there are many varieties of cactus. Sugar apples, papayas, and limes are abundant. Dogwood and white immortelle are two trees in Carriacou unknown in Grenada. The southern mockingbird, the Antillean grackle, and the banaquit are the most common birds (the banaquit is in the yellow phase, which is rare in Grenada). Among others to be seen are glossy cowbirds, ramiers, ground doves, wood doves, kingbirds, elaenias, emerald-throated hummingbirds, and frigate birds. Not often seen but occasionally heard is the mangrove cuckoo.

NOTEWORTHY

Sandy Island, just off Carriacou, is a wonderful place for snorkeling and picnicking. Other nearby islets are the Sisters, Mabouya, and Jack-A-Dan.

Carriacou Museum, on a side street off Main in Hillsborough, has an interesting collection of Amerindian and

European artifacts. Small and friendly, this little museum is a rarity for such a small island.

Tyrrel Bay, on the west side, is a spectacular enclosed bay where the water is always calm and serene. Paradise Beach is a favorite for locals, and the swimming here is excellent.

WHERE TO STAY

Silver Beach Resort
Carriacou, Grenada, West Indies
Telephone: (809) 443-7337
Local islanders, the Bullen family, own and manage this small, friendly resort. There are four duplex cottages (some with kitchens) that face the dining area and beach. Your waitress will most likely be singing when she carries your breakfast to your front veranda. The swimming is excellent in front of the hotel, and to the left it is a five-minute walk to the center of Hillsborough town. On the right, at the end of the beach, is a footpath that rises above the beach and hugs the coastline for a very pleasant walk at sunset. Rates start at $65 single and $80 double.

The Mermaid Inn
Hillsborough, Carriacou, Grenada, West Indies
Telephone: (809) 443-7484
Formerly a private house, The Mermaid Inn is now an eleven-room beachfront inn on the opposite edge of town from Silver Beach Resort. Some of the rooms have four-poster beds and overlook a small courtyard where meals

are served on the water's edge. The staff is very pleasant, and your fellow visitors are often down-islanders from Grenada. Rates are $40 single and $50 double.

Caribbee Inn (formerly Prospect Lodge)

Prospect, Carriacou, Grenada, West Indies
Telephone: (809) 443-7380
On a hill 200 yards above the sea, and on the edge of a proposed national park, Caribbee Inn is restful and quiet. Robert and Wendy Cooper offer comfortable, spacious suites with traditional four-poster beds, good food, a library, snorkel gear, small locally made boats, helpful advice, and local guides. The apartment, a self-contained unit with bedroom, kitchen, bath, and a private porch, has the best view. Orchard Cottage, in a separate building, has two bedrooms, kitchen, and bath. Rates started at $70 double.

Unicey Braveboy

Lauriston, Carriacou, Grenada, West Indies
Telephone: (809) 443-7471
For the traveler on a budget, Unicey Braveboy runs a guest house in Lauriston, facing the quiet road and beach. There is a communal bathroom and kitchen, and rates begin at $18 per day.

Melonie's Villa

Windward Village, Carriacou, Grenada, West Indies
Telephone: (809) 443-7227; New York (718) 493-5383
This unpretentious stone villa is actually two buildings that can accommodate eight adventurous people. The dining/living room is enormous and has one of the most spec-

tacular views in the Caribbean: Petit Martinique, Petit St. Vincent, and Union islands in the distance. The long access road has been newly graded but remains unpaved, sometimes a problem in the rain. A native of Carriacou, Andrew Fleary, lives in New York but returns to his house as often as he can save the airfare to do so. In the interim, he rents both buildings for $850 a week, which includes maid service.

NOTE: When writing for reservations, keep in mind that mail can take two weeks in each direction.

OTHER HOUSE RENTALS

The Grange
Meldrum, Carriacou
Telephone: (809) 443-7467

Fair Winds
Meldrum, Carriacou
Telephone: (809) 443-7333

Peace and Love
Bay a Leau, Carriacou
Telephone: (809) 443-7333

RESTAURANTS

Tip Top Restaurant and Bar, on Main Street, is known for its good local dishes.

Roof Gardens Restaurant and Bar faces the jetty and market, featuring seafood and local foods.

Cassada Bay offers West Indian cuisine, specializing in lobster, oysters, conch, and fish.

The Italian Restaurant on a hill overlooking Tyrrel Bay is quaint and homey and serves fine Italian food.

FROM MY JOURNAL

This morning I was in New York; tonight I've walked a quiet road on Carriacou. Not a single car passed by, only the sound of ocean waves, and the occasional call of a night bird. The fragrant aromas and stillness are overwhelming. What a contrast to New York in July. I may never leave Carriacou!

HOW TO GET THERE

LIAT flies from Barbados and Grenada, and interisland boats travel from St. Vincent and Grenada. *Alexia II* leaves St. George's on Grenada at 10 a.m. on Wednesday and Saturday, and returns from Hillsborough wharf at 10 a.m. on Monday and Thursday.

Petit Martinique

The extinct volcanic peak of Petit Martinique rises dramatically from the sea, a beckoning Bali Hai to those on nearby Carriacou. From the village of Windward, it is easy to arrange a boat for the thirty-minute, three-mile trip across varying shades of blue water to the reef-protected island.

Veralyn "Ann" Jones, a beautiful and intelligent lady from New York, joined me on the boat trip to Petit Martinique. For her, this first visit was extremely special. Her father, John Jones, was born on this quiet island of 600 industrious black inhabitants.

On arrival, the beach was a hub of boating activity—painting, polishing, and other last-minute preparations for the annual regatta. There are no paved roads and no cars on the island, so it was easy to discover this charming, quiet island by foot.

NOTEWORTHY

The hike to the top of Petit Martinique's highest peak affords a spectacular view of the surrounding islands: Petit

St. Vincent, Carriacou, Union, Canouan, and several uninhabited islands.

WHERE TO STAY

Mrs. Petroilla Ceasar
Petit Martinique via Carriacou, Grenada, West Indies
The only rooms and food on the island are available at this
tiny, friendly gathering place.

Union Island

The flight from Carriacou to Union Island takes just five minutes, barely time to marvel at the islands below: Petit Martinique, Petit St. Vincent, and Palm Island. The landing over the harbor town of Clifton, with white sailboats shining on the glimmering azure sea, is spectacular; it passes so quickly that you long for a slow-motion rerun.

The picturesque airport building is an international arrival point to the St. Vincent Grenadines, but rarely do more than two or three passengers enter here from neighboring Carriacou in the Grenada Grenadines. The immigration officer is delighted to see a new arrival to his island, and with passport shown and duly stamped, the visitor is free to leave. The unusual, mountainous beauty of Union is immediately overwhelming.

The plane has departed for Mustique, and the stillness of the island adds to the allure of its tropical remoteness. Mount Taboi rises to 1,000 feet on one side, and on the other is the sea. Here on Union there is no traffic, there are no screeching motorbikes, no buses, no taxis. A grassy path lined with conch shells shows the way across the runway to the Anchorage Hotel. From there along the waterfront and beach, it is a five-minute walk to Clifton town, comprised of several general stores, markets, a minuscule tourist office, two small, locally owned hotels, a few bars and restaurants, and shops selling local handicrafts.

Union Island is a hiker's paradise. The walks are many, and all are rewarding. Crossing the island to the north are Richmond Bay and Belmont Bay. The English-speaking inhabitants along the way are friendly, as are the ubiquitous, well-behaved brown goats.

NOTEWORTHY

Chatham Bay is a beautiful and sequestered bay on the east coast, with excellent swimming.

Frigate Island, part of the Lagoon Reef that protects almost the entire south coast, is an ideal place for snorkeling.

WHERE TO STAY

Anchorage Yacht Club
Clifton, Union Island
St. Vincent Grenadines
Telephone: (809) 458-8244
The five rooms in a coconut grove facing the sea are extremely comfortable, and another five are upstairs in the main building overlooking the tasteful outdoor dining area. This is a French-owned hotel, and the clientele is international and chic. Scuba lessons and equipment are available. Rates start at $65 single and $90 for two.

Sunny Grenadines Hotel
Clifton, Union Island
St. Vincent Grenadines
Telephone: (809) 458-8327
King Mitchell, a retired Union Island seaman, welcomes travelers to his informal waterfront hotel set in a quiet garden. The duplex units facing the sea are the ones to request. Mr. Mitchell is happy to arrange inexpensive boat trips to Tobago Cays (excellent snorkeling) and neighboring islands. Rates start at $40 single and $50 for two.

Clifton Beach Hotel
Clifton, Union Island
St. Vincent Grenadines
Telephone: (809) 458-8235
There are ten rooms with private baths facing the beach of Clifton town harbor. The rooms are spartan but comfortable, and the staff is friendly. Clifton Beach Hotel is also owned by a local islander, Conrad Adams. Rates start at $30 single and $40 double.

Travelers on a tight budget will be warmly welcomed at the Clifton Beach Guest House in Clifton town.

RESTAURANTS

The only food on Union Island is served at your guest house or hotel.

FROM MY JOURNAL

Today I was asked for the third time whether I was a priest. I facetiously answered in Latin, thus establishing my reputation for my one remaining day on Union Island. On inquiry I learned it was not my round glasses, white shirt, or the Panama hat that tipped them off; it was my manner of rushing around with important business to do! Hilarious visions of Jacques Tati on Union Island came to mind. I decided it was time to move more leisurely and less conspicuously on to the next island.

HOW TO GET THERE

There is air service on LIAT from Barbados, St. Vincent, Grenada, and Carriacou, and on Air Martinique to points north—St. Vincent, Dominica, and Martinique. The local boat from St. Vincent leaves at 10 a.m. on Monday and Thursday and returns on Tuesday and Friday (see ferry schedule at the end of the Grenadines chapter).

    NOTE: Save money for the departure tax when you leave Union (St. Vincent Grenadines) for Carriacou (Grenada Grenadines).

Mayreau

The 100 inhabitants of quiet Mayreau are devout Roman Catholics, and I was grateful to have preceded my own "priestly" reputation. Dropped off as the sole departing passenger of the sailing vessel *United Knowledge*, I walked slowly up the path away from the beach. I felt the centuries dissolve as the *United Knowledge* disappeared around a distant point and I was alone to discover the tranquil beauty of the island. Mayreau is small—only one-and-a-half square miles—yet on foot it seems much larger. There are no roads and no cars. There are goats, sheep, virgin beaches, the land, and the sea. The vistas are exceptional, and from the church above the village there is a spectacular panorama of Canouan, Union, Tobago Cays, Petit St. Vincent, and Grenada.

Life on Mayreau revolves around the sea, fishing, and sailing. The wooden houses are small but not without character, and many have small subsistence vegetable gardens. A true sense of community pervades the island. Everyone meets for mass in the charming stone Catholic church with its magnificent view. In this very quiet, rural island existence, no one goes without if help is needed.

Rarely will you see another person on the beaches—
perhaps a fisherman or occasionally a visiting yachtsman
who has anchored in Salt Whistle Bay. To stay overnight or
for a few days offers an experience rarely felt in the twentieth century.

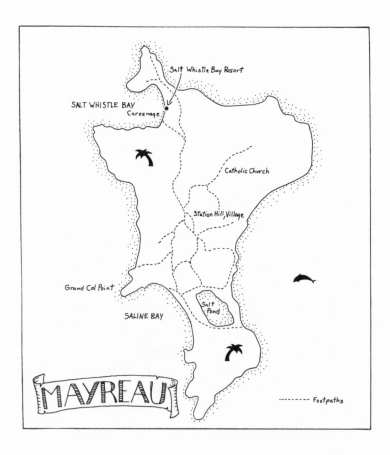

NOTEWORTHY

The walk across the island's lowland to the windward side is worth taking. In the dry season there are intricate crystals of rock salt in an original salt pond, and on the beach there are shells and interesting driftwood.

The Tobays Cays (excellent snorkeling) are just thirty minutes away by sailboat.

WHERE TO STAY

Salt Whistle Bay Club
Mayreau via Union Island
St. Vincent Grenadines
Telephone: (416) 430-1275, 1-212-535-9530
Fax: (416) 430-8988
Salt Whistle Bay provides the island's only overnight accommodations and food. This small, expensive resort is well hidden among the trees on the beach facing Salt Whistle Bay.

HOW TO GET THERE

The interisland ferry will make a stop at Mayreau when requested to do so. The Salt Whistle Bay Club will meet guests by private launch at nearby Union Island.

Canouan

Waiting for the small launch to arrive for the move from schooner to shore, one can tell even before setting foot on Canouan that it is a beach lover's paradise. On this quiet island, the beaches are long, empty, and incredibly white against the calm turquoise sea.

On shore, the island is brown and rather barren in the lowland and yet very green and tropical on the hills. The jungle casts its shadow on the end of Grand Bay and turns the water an emerald green for a never-to-be-forgotten swim at sunset.

Fishing, farming, and sailing occupy most of the island's 700 shy but friendly English-speaking inhabitants. The roads are not paved, and only very occasionally will you need to step aside for a passing jeep.

NOTEWORTHY

On the island's east side there are many excellent deserted beaches and coves that are easy to reach in less than an hour by foot. A deserted old church is all that remains of a village swept away by a hurricane in 1921.

WHERE TO STAY

Crystal Sands Hotel
Canouan, St. Vincent Grenadines
Telephone: (809) 458-8015
Natives of Canouan own and manage this five-duplex cottage resort. The rooms are very basic, each with private bath and paper-thin walls. But if you get one of the three

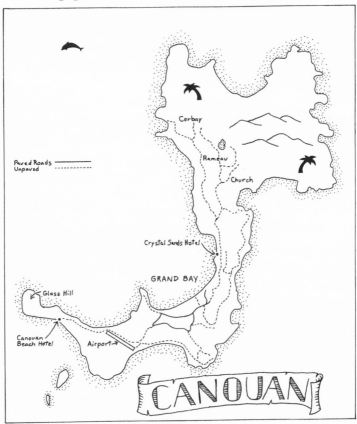

cottages directly on the beach, you will be so entranced with the location, excellent swimming, and friendly fellow guests (usually islanders from St. Vincent) that any inconvenience will quickly be forgotten. Rates start at $50 single and $80 double, including breakfast and dinner.

Canouan Beach Hotel
P.O. Box 530
Canouan, St. Vincent Grenadines
Telephone: (809) 458-8888
This is the hotel that old-time visitors to Canouan felt was inevitable and that one day would spoil this tranquil island. Built on the other side of the island from Crystal Sands, the new hotel is so inconspicuous that a visitor could sail by and miss it entirely. It is French owned, and the international clientele enjoy a wide variety of water sports, snorkeling, and swimming off magnificent, uncrowded beaches. Rates start at $90 single and $170 double, including three meals.

For visitors on a limited budget, Le Bijou Guest House has six basic rooms on the beach. Breakfast and dinner are included in the $25 single and $50 double rates.

FROM MY JOURNAL

Lots of sun on this dry island. Took a quick shower and thought that this lack of abundant water is a small price to pay to safeguard Canouan from overdevelopment. We few visitors who do arrive bring contact with the outside world

and new jobs for the young, who would otherwise leave the island.

HOW TO GET THERE

Boat service from St. Vincent leaves on Monday and Thursday around 9 a.m. and arrives on Canouan in the afternoon. The boat returns on Tuesday and Friday. Air Martinique has flights from St. Vincent.

PRACTICAL TIPS

Immigration: For Carriacou and Petit Martinique, passports are not required of United States citizens provided they have two proofs of citizenship (one with photo) and a return air ticket. A driver's license with a photo and an original birth certificate will suffice. Be advised that if you visit the St. Vincent Grenadines (Mayreau, Canouan, and Union), you will need a passport. There is a $25 EC (US$9) departure tax when returning to the United States from the Grenada Grenadines and $15 EC ($6) from the St. Vincent Grenadines.

Currency: The Eastern Caribbean (EC) dollar is used on all the Grenadine Islands. The exchange rate is approximately EC $2.60 to US$1.

Language: The official language is English.

VENEZUELA

Isla de Coche

Within view of the overdeveloped, heavily touristed Venezuelan resort destination of Isla Margarita lies a remarkable opportunity to get away from it all. Just a 90-minute ferryboat ride or a twenty-minute airplane flight from the frantic commercial bustle of Isla Margarita, Isla de Coche offers little more than a supremely tranquil setting for stress-free relaxation at shockingly affordable prices. The relatively flat and arid island is home to a thousand or so residents who depend upon fishing or intermittent salt manufacturing operations for their living. Tourist development is virtually nonexistent—no T-shirts or souvenirs—and it is primarily vacationers from Caracas who cross over from Margarita to check out the absolute peace and quiet of this hidden oasis. But for the adventurous traveler who is looking only for a restful setting to enjoy the sea, the sun, and delicious native cooking, Coche is a rugged chunk of paradise.

Our first sighting of Isla de Coche from the large passenger ferry that cruises over from Punta de Piedras on Margarita was ambiguous. From this northerly approach, the island appears to be mostly deserted, with a few strange buildings materializing into view. Drawing closer, we saw a string of houses near the long beach to the left of the ferry landing. They are part of a failed housing development near the salt extraction facilities. A huge, concrete, institutional-looking structure on the hill turns out to be the largest of the island's many churches. Far to the right, on the western tip of the island, a lonely stand of palm trees marks the foreigner's likely destination, Coche's only accommodation, the Hotel Turistico.

Initially, the island has a strangely desolate feeling. One or two taxis are waiting at the dock to take passengers on the short trip into San Pedro de Coche, the island's main village. The ride winds through dusty streets, past ramshackle buildings and cinder block housing in various states of construction and disrepair. But once settled into the hotel, with a cool drink and a friendly welcome from the young staff, the foreboding feeling of landing in an alien environment, where few tourists tread, melts into welcome sighs of relaxation. Upon arrival at the hotel, when our limited traveler's repertoire of Spanish was failing us, a visiting airline pilot set aside his coffee and tried to interpret with his limited English. Before long, several guests had joined in. Within a few hours we had made new acquaintances and discovered ways to communicate relatively clearly with our hosts (who turned out to speak plenty of English).

Coche's main appeal is the chance to escape from civilization into a culture that is virtually oblivious to the hyperactivity of mainland life. Add to that the warm and accommodating nature of the hotel staff and the other guests (almost all Venezuelan), and what seemed alien

becomes comfortable and familiar. The daily life of Coche —the repair of fishing nets and boats, the early morning launches, the preparation of the catch, the late afternoon games in the streets or on the beaches—goes on undisturbed by the trickle of visitors.

Our first walk through the puebla of San Pedro drew silent stares from curious children and bemused adults who rarely see North Americans on their streets. We felt like we had landed from another planet. After exploring the quiet streets of San Pedro, we decided to find a way to investigate the rest of the island. For about 100 bolivars an hour (less than $3), a driver will take you around the entire island: through the smaller villages of Guinima, Guamache, and El Bichar; out past the airport and the salt-processing sheds; along the vast white beach at Punta La Playa. If you are lucky, you will hear stories about how the islanders drove a Catholic priest off Coche because he offended their traditional sensibilities. Taking us back to the 5 a.m. ferry on the morning of our departure, our driver, Bertrand, related how he had been visited by spirits in the night, both on the road to Guinima and in his own home. They took the form of nuns and young girls, he said, except for one old woman spirit who is known as "the quiet one."

Our finest hours on Coche were spent swimming in the calm Caribbean waters in the early morning before the considerable heat of noon, or at dusk, when the air is like velvet and large sea birds slant against the crimson and orange cloud-dappled sky. At night, an unbelievable calm descends with the darkness, even as the evening breezes pick up and rattle the few palms. Sleep comes easily with the gentle rhythms of the waves upon the shore. All the cares you left behind melt away as Coche reminds you how to lose yourself in the long, peaceful moment.

NOTEWORTHY

Punta la Playa is the location of Coche's finest beach, a long arc of white sand around a cove of warm, shallow water. Other than the small beach at the hotel, this is the easiest place to swim. While you can have immense sections of beach all to yourself, be sure to either bring your own shade (the playa is treeless) or avoid the hot midday hours. Other rockier spots on Coche's shore are excellent for shell collecting.

The Panaderia, two blocks away from the hotel, is a large, relatively modern market providing fresh breads, cold drinks, bottled water, and various canned and dry goods.

Local fishermen make their boats available for hire. They can take you to the nearby island of Cubagua or to various locations for fishing and snorkeling. Remember, there are no regular tourist services, such as dive shops on Coche, so it is up to you to find locals who can help you shape your own vacation. The Hotel Turistico staff knows many such islanders.

WHERE TO STAY

Hotel Turistico
San Pedro de Coche
Isla de Coche, Venezuela
Telephone: (095) 9-9177
Once you have arrived on Isla de Coche, just ask your taxi

VENEZUELA

driver to take you to "the hotel." Located on the western end of the island, at the northwestern corner of the main village of San Pedro, the Hotel Turistico is the only game in town. But this adequately maintained sixteen-room hotel does not exploit its position with high rates and careless service. Subsidized by the Venezuelan government, the hotel is operated by two young men, Miguel and Jesus, who see after the guests with charming enthusiasm. The rooms are right on the beach with direct views of the beautiful Caribbean sunsets. While the accommodations are relatively spartan—whitewashed walls, red-tile floors, ceiling fans, minimal furniture, and only cold water in the bathrooms—they are clean and very reasonably priced. In the octagonal bar, the walls are decorated with felt marker graffiti and signatures of the hotel's guests, and loud Caribbean and American pop music often blares out of the stereo. The adjoining octagonal dining room looks out on the beach's and the island's only stand of palm trees. Once you have settled into the slow, carefree rhythms of life on Coche, the hotel quickly becomes a relaxing home, and the guests and employees begin to feel like family. Rates are about $8 a night for a single, just under $10 for a double.

RESTAURANTS

Although San Pedro de Coche does have a few tiny bars and markets, the only place for travelers to eat is the Hotel Turistico. The food is excellent. Local women prepare delicious soups with fresh fish, shrimp, and crabs; *arepas* (a fried dough that is sometimes slightly sweet); rice and black beans; fried bananas; and a variety of fish and chicken dishes. The best dinners feature tomato and cheese salads, *tostones* (fried plantain), and *pargo*, a local fish related to grouper and snapper, grilled with garlic. Miguel and Jesus run a full bar, assisted by Orpheo, who speaks excellent English. One night they surprised us by cutting up a fresh cantaloupe and mixing it with crushed ice in a blender for a delicious and refreshing fruit drink. Two people can eat and drink well for less than $10 a day.

FROM MY JOURNAL

The door of our small room faces the sea. The sun is hovering above the silver horizon, trying to decide whether to set. The palm trees are black silhouettes against an orange sky. Children and parents have come to the beach from the village and the nearby fishing huts. Some are swimming, others playing soccer in the sand. A few guests have set up a makeshift volleyball game. A gentle breeze is rustling the palm leaves against the window. The water is like velvet. We look around and see a dozen other bodies half submerged in the warm tide, all motionless, all turned west, away from the beach, staring toward the radiant sunset that is making great pink and purple streaks across the sky.

HOW TO GET THERE

Avensa Air and Linea Aeropostal Venezolana operate scheduled flights from Caracas (Maiquetia Airport) to Isla Margarita. The ferry to Coche departs from Punta de Piedras Monday through Thursday at 12:30 p.m., on Friday and Saturday at 10:30 a.m., and on Sundays at 8 a.m., 1:30 p.m., and 5:30 p.m. But note that schedules can change, and be sure to inquire, preferably in Spanish, at the terminal about the current times. The fare is about 50 cents.

Aero Taxi el Sol de America runs flights from Margarita to Coche twice daily, at 8 a.m. and 4:30 p.m., for about $6 per person. But check ahead of time, because the service is not always in operation.

Isla de Cubagua

To the east of Isla de Coche lies the smaller island of Isla de Cubagua. The site of the first Spanish city in Venezuela and once the locale of rich pearl fisheries, Cubagua is now a barren and windswept desert island. On Coche, you can hear stories about how the Spaniards mercilessly enslaved and murdered the original Indian population and how that original city was swept away centuries ago by a monstrous storm. On Cubagua, you can walk through the rubble of stone that makes up the "ruins" of the early settlement. The only signs of life today are a few shacks used by local fishermen and a small marine laboratory on one of the bays. The island itself is flat and scrubby, its vegetation dominated by several varieties of blooming cactus.

The only way to get to Cubagua is to hire a fishing boat on Coche. Felipe, who lives across the street from the Panaderia, will take you in his partially covered inboard-engine boat for between $15 and $20. You need to leave early in the morning so that you can return before the sea gets rough in the afternoon. The ride takes about an hour and fifteen minutes. Two or three hours are enough to explore the ruins, beachcomb, and swim and snorkel around the reefs. The wreck of an old ferry marks the entrance to Ensenada de Charagato. Large gray pelicans roost on the rusted hull. In the quiet bay, sailboats anchor for shelter. It is a fine spot for swimming and shelling, with a smooth sandy beach. On shore, fishermen offered to sell us fresh lobster, but we opted for a shell with a small pearl developing on its inner wall. A truly adventurous soul could probably camp for the night on Cubagua, but a day trip is enough for a glimpse of a place where the distant past and the present are not very far apart.

PRACTICAL TIPS

Immigration: A passport, but not a visa, is required for entrance into Venezuela.

Currency: The Venezuelan currency is based on the bolivar (B). When the exchange rate is favorable to the dollar, at about 43 B to the dollar, prices are outrageously low: coffee for about 3 cents, soft drinks for about 12 cents. On the way to Coche, the best place to exchange currency is right in the Maiquetia Airport.

If your schedule requires that you spend time on Isla Margarita, take best advantage of your time by enjoying one of the excellent restaurants in Porlamar—such as O Sole Mio Restaurant da Rosetta at Calle Cedeno y Calle Malave, or Restaurant Martin Pescador—that serve enormous portions of delicious lobster in elegant settings at bargain prices.

BELIZE

The cays of Belize are the most hospitable and accessible of all the islands along the coast of Central America. Formerly British Honduras and now a member of the British Commonwealth as an independent democratic nation, Belize is unique among Central American countries. It is an uncrowded country of only fifteen inhabitants per square mile. When the nonprofit Freedom House Foundation ranked countries according to their respect for human rights and civil liberties, it grouped Belize with Britain, Canada, and the United States. It is a safe and stable country with a literacy rate over 90 percent. The friendly and hospitable English-speaking inhabitants welcome visitors warmly and are striving to develop a tourist industry to boost their declining sugar-based economy.

Although primitive in some ways, Belize is both healthy and safe. Water is drinkable almost everywhere, and inoculations are not needed. For a poor country, there is a remarkable lack of both theft and panhandling. The people are friendly, helpful, and proud.

There are 175 islands off the coast of Belize! These beautiful cays (pronounced "keys") are flat, narrow, beach-

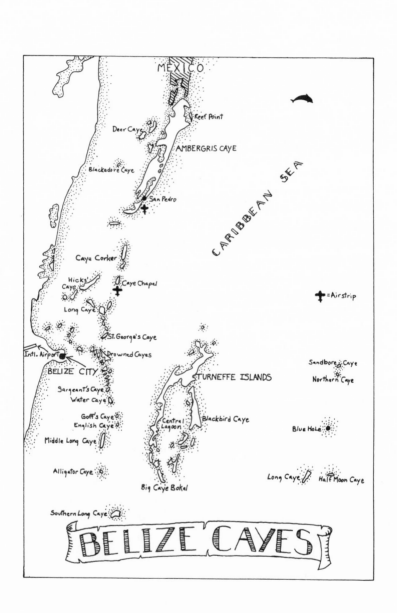

BELIZE CAYES

lined islands that are mostly populated by an incredible variety of birds. Less than a dozen cays have any human inhabitants, and aside from several privately owned resort islands and various research stations, only three cays offer the visitor overnight accommodations. No other island group in the Caribbean has a larger or more spectacular barrier reef than Belize's, which is second in size only to the Great Barrier Reef of Australia.

Ambergris Cay, sharing a border with Mexico's Yucatán, is the most developed, yet it remains quiet and off the beaten track. Just south is Cay Caulker (pronounced and sometimes spelled "Caye Corker"). This island is even more secluded, a veritable bargain paradise where one can stay for as little as $10 a night or "splurge" on a hearty lobster dinner for $5! St. George's Caye is home to a few residents, a twelve-room hand-built lodge, and four thatched-roof cottages. The largest number of guests ever on the island at one time was twenty-eight. There are several lodges on private cays: Turneffe Island Lodge on Caye Bokel; Lomont's on North East and Longe cays; Pyramid Island Resort on Cay Chapel; and the Wave Reef Resort on Gallows Point Caye. These isolated lodges are known only to the most avid scuba divers and fishermen, who have found these waters to be among the world's finest diving and fishing destinations.

If time allows, visits to the Mayan sites of Xunantunich and Altun Ha on the mainland are richly rewarding. Belize is a natural wonder, supporting over 500 species of exotic birds and 250 varieties of orchids, and it is one of the last stands of the elusive jaguar.

Ambergris Caye

The small, comfortable hotels that have opened in the last decade on Ambergris have not spoiled the sleepy atmosphere of this 35-mile-long island. There may now be an air-conditioned luxury hotel or two, but the streets— Front, Middle, and Back—remain nothing more than hard-packed white sand. Automobiles are still rare.

San Pedro, the only town, has a white, dusty frontier look about it. The wooden buildings are parched and weathered by the salt and searing sun. Fishing still remains the island's chief concern, but tourism has brought employment and income to many who otherwise would have left the island. After a bountiful catch, picturesque fishing boats line the waterfront of San Pedro town. Fresh fish grilled to perfection is one of the joys of an Ambergris stay.

Here on Ambergris, the reef is less than a mile offshore, and the waves can be seen breaking easily along it. The pristine and virgin quality of the reef make it one of the world's best diving locations. Massive coral canyons at depths of 50 to 100 feet can be explored along the main barrier reef. Each canyon is full of caves and tunnels teeming with life, and it is not unusual to see a school of porpoises or huge turtles swimming along beside you.

For the novice snorkeler or swimmer, the area inside the reef is rarely deeper than forty feet. Calm and protected, the water is a wonderland of brilliantly colored fish of fluorescent orange and purple, dazzling red and green, and electric blue. Above this boundless aquarium, constant breezes provide ideal conditions for sailing and windsurfing.

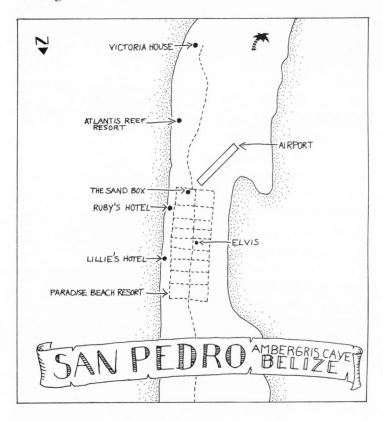

Time moves slowly on Ambergris. Dogs sleep at high noon on the sandy main street. Toward evening they amble aside for the San Pedro youngsters, who play softball. Fishing, swimming, snorkeling, scuba diving, sailing, eating, reading, sleeping; there is much to be said for this island's lazy and rejuvenating way of life.

NOTEWORTHY

Hol Chan Marine Reserve, a 4½-square-mile area at the south end of the Caye, opened as a national park in May 1987. This spectacular area has been set aside for the protection and observation of marine life and will become a major spawning area for hundreds of fish species.

WHERE TO STAY

Paradise Hotel
San Pedro, Ambergris Caye, Belize
Telephone: (713) 850-1664 or (800) 537-1431
The Paradise is the nicest hotel right in town. Thatch-roofed cottages are arranged around a beachfront garden with bar and lounge areas. Rates start at $40 single, $65 double, and $100 air-conditioned suites. Excellent food.

Rubie's Hotel
San Pedro, Ambergris Caye, Belize
Telephone: 2-62063
This budget hotel has no air-conditioning and no frills, but it is right on the beach with good ventilation and superb views in two directions. Rates are $20 with private bath and $15 without.

Lily's Caribeña Lodge
San Pedro, Ambergris Caye, Belize
Telephone: 2-62059
Lily's is similar to Rubie's, but some rooms have no views. Access is from the beach or through the backyards of adjoining buildings. The six beachfront rooms have private baths and cost $25 per couple from May-October and $35 from November-April. There is a popular seafood restaurant where meals can be had by advance arrangement.

Victoria House
Ambergris Caye, Belize
Telephone: 2-73041

A few miles south of town, there are ten small thatched-roof *casitas* and six deluxe air-conditioned rooms in the main lodge.

HOUSEKEEPING APARTMENTS

House of the Rising Sun
San Pedro, Ambergris Caye, Belize
These new studios, with full kitchens and ceiling fans, are located on the beach a short distance from San Pedro.

Tropical Travel Representative in Houston, Texas, can reserve and arrange economical air-hotel packages to Rising Sun and all other major accommodations in Belize; telephone: (800) 451-8017.

RESTAURANTS

Elvi's, a sand-floored hut on the center street of town, features inexpensive local seafood with conch and lobster specialties.

Sand Box is a good Mexican restaurant across the road from the airport in San Pedro town.

The Hut, a moderately priced popular restaurant, is noted for its turtle curry. Owner Shelley Prevett provides hard-to-get information (about baby-sitters, air charters, local black-coral jewelry makers, etc.). Shelly's brother, Penny Arceo, is a knowledgeable instructor of bonefishing, snorkeling, diving, and bird-watching.

HOW TO GET THERE

Tan Sahsa Airlines operates nonstop service from Miami (two hours), New Orleans, and Houston. Challenge International and TACA International Airlines also serve Belize City. Allow time in Belize City to switch airports if you intend to fly on Maya or Tropic Air directly to San Pedro (a 20-minute flight that concludes with a landing on the Band-Aid-sized airstrip). It is quite feasible to drive to Belize City from any point in the United States, then leave the car behind for the ferry trip to Ambergris, Caye Caulker, or St. George Caye.

Caye Caulker

A few miles south of Ambergris is less-visited and less-expensive Caye Caulker. The island is so narrow that you can see the water on the other side as you approach one of the little docks that the locals call "bridges." The cay is virtually all beach, and the inhabited portion is so small that one can easily walk its length and breadth within an hour. It is a barefoot island; all the roads and paths are sand, free of rocks and broken glass. After a day or two, one gets to know many of the 450 friendly islanders and the visitors who come from all parts of the world. Local artist Phillip Lewis, whose work decorates the face of Belizean currency, sells his own map of the island which includes everything from where to get a massage to the entrance of the world's largest underwater cave system. Phillip knows everyone and greets visitors as he makes his daily stroll around the island. The friendliness and low prices of Caye Caulker tempt the visitor into long stays.

NOTEWORTHY

Ellen MacRae's Art Gallery: Ellen MacRae is not only a fine graphic artist but also a marine biologist who lectures on reef ecology and bird-watching. If the conditions are right, she will follow her lecture with a guided trip to the reef.

The Cut: This deep channel slices through the island and is an ideal place for swimming, especially since much

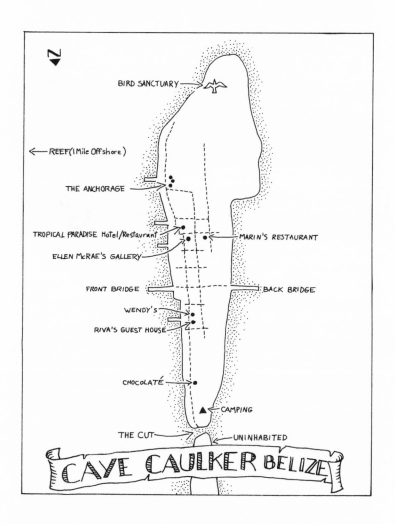

N

BIRD SANCTUARY

←—REEF(1 Mile Offshore)

THE ANCHORAGE

TROPICAL PARADISE Hotel/Restaurant

MARIN'S RESTAURANT

ELLEN McRAE'S GALLERY

FRONT BRIDGE

BACK BRIDGE

WENDY'S

RIVA'S GUEST HOUSE

CHOCOLATÉ

CAMPING

THE CUT

UNINHABITED

CAYE CAULKER BELIZE

of the water around the island is so shallow. It is a local favorite for children, who enjoy the high diving from the branch of an overhanging tree.

WHERE TO STAY

Marin's
Caye Caulker, Belize
There is a very warm welcome at this clean and comfortable courtyard inn. Rooms with private bath start at $23 per couple.

Riva's Guest House
Caye Caulker, Belize
Above the Aberdeen Chinese Restaurant (which serves good food) are six rooms that rent for as little as $10 a night. The rooms are small, spartan, and without private facilities,

but the view from the front porch is as fine as any on the island. You can watch the island population walk by in the evening as you sip a cool drink on the porch, with the colors of the sunset reflected on the blue Caribbean.

Tropical Paradise Hotel and Beach Cottages
Ramon Reyes
Caye Caulker, Belize
Telephone: 2-22124
This is the most expensive place to stay on the island. Rates start at $18 per night and soar to $23 for private bath with hot water. Three new suites will be finished by summer 1990.

RESTAURANTS

Marin's: The delicious lobster, served indoors or out in the garden, is as good as any outside of Maine. Two large tails with hot butter cost only $3.50. They were so tasty that, even though I went back three times, I could never get myself to try anything else!

Tropical Paradise Hotel Restaurant: This is the place to go for breakfast or lunch. You eat in the sunny courtyard or inside, where ceiling fans keep it pleasantly cool. My favorites are their conch fritters, which cost only $1 for a plate of two and are the size of hamburgers and much more satisfying.

Wendy's: Wendy serves breakfast in her tiny cottage. Crêpes with fresh fruit and homemade yogurt, including coffee, cost $2.

HOW TO GET THERE

There is no airfield on Caulker. Morning boats from Belize City make the journey in about an hour and a half. At Mom's Triangle Inn (a famous rendezvous spot), tour and boat information is posted on a bulletin board. Chocolat, who runs a boat every day except Sunday to and from Caye Caulker, can be found eating breakfast there every morning. He charges about $6 for one-way passage on the *Soledad*, his open boat that bounces like a roller coaster as it speeds over the waves. Mangrove Islets appear through the salty spray as the mainland vanishes from view. Coming from nearby Ambergris, you can charter a boat for the short trip.

St. George's Caye

Less than nine miles from Belize City Harbor, St. George's Caye was the first capital of British Honduras, from 1650 to 1784. It is reputed to be the scene of a great sea battle against the Spaniards in 1798. With only a small resident population, the island is much quieter today, and only a few reminders of its past endure. A sandy footpath parallels the coastline from the public pier. The swimming and snorkeling are excellent from any of the seven piers, or "bridges." Most of the spectacular dive sites are only ten to fifteen minutes from the dock of the island's only lodge.

WHERE TO STAY

St. George's Lodge
P.O. Box 625
Belize City, Belize
or
Tropical Travel Representative
720 Worthshire
Houston, TX 77008
Telephone: (713) 869-3614 or (800) 451-8017

The only accommodation on the island is St. George's Lodge, a secluded retreat handcrafted of local hardwoods. The beamed cathedral ceiling and handmade furniture in the public area are unique. The lodge has twelve rooms in the main building and four thatch-roofed cottages built over the ocean. Expensive.

HOW TO GET THERE

Occasional boats from Belize City make the twenty-minute crossing to the public pier, but most visitors are guests at the lodge and are met by private boat.

Outside Belize's barrier reef are three spectacular atolls: ring-shaped coral islands surrounding a lagoon. Rarely found outside the South Pacific, the three in Belizean waters—Lighthouse Reef, Turneffe Reef, and Glover's Reef—are a nature lover's dream. They are far removed from civilization, surrounded by an azure sea teeming with rare and exotic marine life.

Glover's Reef: Long Caye and North East Caye

The Lomont family has lived for twenty years on a group of remote sandy islands 40 miles off the Belize mainland. They welcome adventurous guests to their islands.

Long Caye, located on the edge of a 2,000-foot drop-off, is 2,000 feet long and 500 feet wide, formed of coral and white sand piled up as high as ten feet on the reef. According to the earliest maps, it was already well planted with coconut trees in 1700. Seven rustic rental cabins that have been built on the beach overlooking the coral reef are well suited to the intrepid ocean and sun lover seeking a remote, quiet spot "at the end of the world."

North East Caye, comprising nine acres, is even more secluded than Long Caye and is at the center of a wilderness area, part of the proposed Glover's Reef Underwater Park. In order not to disturb the birds, fish, and nesting turtles, there are no motors, bright lights, or loud music. Three double guest cabins, a caretaker's house, and kitchen are the only structures on the island. Rowboats and canoes are available, and snorkeling around here is excellent.

WHERE TO STAY

Glover's Reef Atoll Resort
Box 563
Belize City, Belize
Telephone: 2-44505

The seven cabins on Long Caye are built on stilts at 50-foot intervals for total privacy. Each has two beds, a kitchen corner with utensils, kerosene stove and lanterns, veranda with hammocks, downstairs sun-warmed shower and outhouse. These rustic cabins and the three on North East Caye are $25 a night per couple.

HOW TO GET THERE

A taxi will meet you at the Belize City Airport, stop at fruit and vegetable stores, then take you to Sittee River via a jungle road. Here you will stay overnight in a simple cabin by the river and eat with a local family. The boat leaves on Sunday morning. Depending on the weather and the number of passengers, the crossing will either be taken aboard a skiff (2 to 4 hours), a 26-foot sloop with outboard (6 to 7 hours), or a 50-foot diesel sailing boat (4 to 5 hours). The boat returns on Friday afternoon.

Turneffe Reef: Caye Bokel

Caye Bokel is 12.4 acres of sand beach and coconut palms. Turneffe Diving Lodge has long operated here as a very small, first-rate fishing camp. Scuba diving is now included, as there is excellent diving within ten minutes of the island's dock. Sites include the wreck of the *Sayonara*, the Majestic Reef (with black coral trees in fifty feet of water), the Elbow, and Half-Moon Caye. The lodge's boat meets guests in Belize City.

NOTEWORTHY

Lighthouse Reef: Less than two hours by boat from Caye Bokel, the Lighthouse Reef is an uninhabited chain visited only by the most adventurous divers. The Blue Hole, the mysterious underwater shaft explored by Jacques Cousteau, is more than 400 feet deep and features magnificent stalactite formations.

PRACTICAL TIPS

Immigration: A valid passport and onward ticket are required for entry to Belize. There is a $10 (BZ$20) departure tax.

Currency: The monetary unit is the Belizean dollar stabilized at BZ$2 = US$1.

Language: The official language is English.

Mosquitoes and small insects might be a problem at certain times of the year. Jungle Juice, Cutter's, or Avon Bath Oil are good deterrents. Most insects cannot fly when there is a breeze, so a fan can be useful at night.

WEST CARIBBEAN

Isla Mujeres

Change comes slowly to Isla Mujeres. Although the "Island of Women" is just a short boat ride away from the plastic glamor and programmed vacationland of Cancún, it resists the invasion of time-share condos and tennis courts. Isla Mujeres may be one of the least hidden of the Caribbean's hidden islands, as more and more North Americans and Europeans discover its charms, but it still exists as a world apart from the luxury hotels and designer luggage across the water.

The narrow, five-mile-long island sustains an extraordinary balance of tourism and the authentic indigenous life of a Mexican fishing village. Although large parties of Cancúnites cruise over on tour boats for day trips of snorkeling and buffets, they usually stay away from the town in their preplanned outings. And while certain omens of modernization have crept in—satellite television dishes at a few bars, air-conditioning in several hotels—there are small signs of deferred progress: small plane service from the Cancún airport to the Isla Mujeres army base airstrip seems to have been discontinued, and the boldest attempt at a high-rise luxury hotel is already looking a bit weather-beaten in its isolated location at the northern tip of the island. New construction proceeds very slowly, and it is visually offset by the older, timeworn architecture and tempered by the leisurely pace of life determined by geography and climate. So Isla Mujeres is not overwhelmed by rampant growth, and its attractions of gorgeous beaches, bountiful fishing, and, if Jacques Cousteau is to be taken at his word, some of the best snorkeling in the world can be enjoyed in a relatively serene atmosphere.

The island is accessible by ferry boats from two different mainland locations. From the fishing village of Puerto Juárez, five miles north of Cancún, a passenger ferry leaves for Isla Mujeres about every two hours throughout the day. Three miles farther north, at Punta Sam, an auto ferry, which also carries passengers without vehicles, makes the trip on a slightly less frequent basis. Although you can drive around the island, there are few places to go of any considerable distance, and transportation is cheap and abundant; taxi fares are regulated, and small motorbikes are available by the hour or the day. So there is no compelling reason to make the trip with an automobile.

At Puerto Juárez, a small information booth is located at the wharf, where you can obtain information about the next departure. You might be offered passage on a private boat, but the fare is likely to be seven or eight times the cost of the ferry. On the dock, vendors sell succulent fruits from pushcarts, such as apples and mangoes peeled and carved into the shapes of flowers. Along the shoreline, donkeys bray in nearby yards and exotic birds screech in the palms.

Like an oversized version of the *African Queen*, the large wooden boat chugs in across the calm waters and ties

up to the dock. For a half-hour or so, passengers climb on board and settle onto the wooden benches. On one trip you are likely to hear four or five different languages, perhaps including French, German, and Swedish as well as Spanish and English, reflecting the diversity of the mostly youthful tourists mixed with local commuters. Young Mexican men and women load on large bundles of locally produced hammocks, piñatas, and other handicrafts, for sale on the island. Already, as the boat sets off on its 45-minute voyage across the sea, the slightly crazed rush of arriving in Cancún and hustling to Puerto Juárez has subsided, melting into the soothing, warm, and salty breeze.

Isla Mujeres was named by Spanish explorers in 1517. Impressed by the many female icons they found on the island, the conquistadors called it "Island of Women."

Today, the last remaining vestige of the original Mayan civilization is a small temple ruin at the rocky, southern-

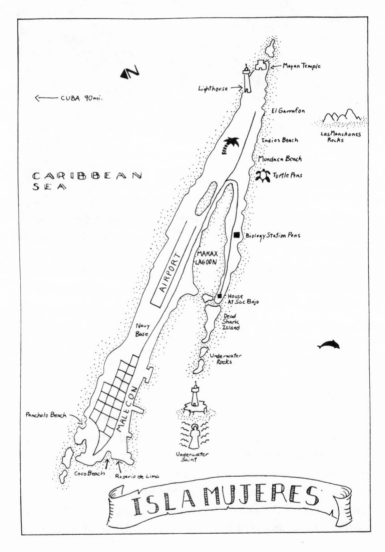

most tip. As you approach the island by ferry, however, the evidence of modernism gathers shape on the northwestern shore, where the hotels, restaurants, and tourist shops are crowded together amidst the houses and shops of the island population. Tall palm trees rise up around the densely constructed town, enhancing the exotic image of the island, which is otherwise fairly flat and covered mostly by scrubby jungle.

At the landing, the commotion of tourists, taxis, and vendors can be initially intimidating. The taxi stand is located next to the dock, but almost all the restaurants and hotels are within walking distance. During the tourist season, it is wise to make reservations in advance. Otherwise, Isla Mujeres offers a full range of accommodations. Several medium-priced hotels, such as the Vistal Mar, and more expensive modern hotels, like the Posada del Mar, are located along the Avenida Rueda Medina, which runs from the pier along the western beachfront. Toward the northern tip of the island, near the snow-white sands of Playa Los Cocos, are the inexpensive, concrete and thatched-roof bungalows of the Cabañas Zazil-Ha, while farther around the island's tip, past Playa Norte, stands the beautifully located but pretentiously designed and surprisingly non-luxurious 100-room Hotel El Presidente Caribe. Two resort hotels are situated out of town, down the western coast: Maria's, with romantic pink stucco bungalows around a shady palm garden and offering a French restaurant with outdoor dining; and Hacienda Gomar, an ambitious complex with shops, hotel rooms, and a large dining room and terrace near the beach.

For the least expensive, centrally located hotels, follow one of the narrow streets (Aves. Morelos and Bravo) straight ahead from the pier. In the interior of town, you'll find a variety of small, inexpensive, and moderately priced hotels—the Hotels Martinez, Berny, Osorio, Caracol, and Caribe Maya, for instance—some with air-conditioning, others with only ceiling fans. On the eastern, rocky side of the island, only a three-block walk, two hotels overlook the rough surf of the ocean: the newer Rocas del Caribe, and the slightly older, more picturesque Hotel Rocamar, perched on a high corner of town right above the town square.

Once settled, you can start your explorations of the island. The town, just a few blocks wide and only slightly longer, readily becomes familiar. Street names are of little use, but it's virtually impossible to get lost, as you quickly learn such major reference points as the pier, the *zócalo* (town square), the lighthouse tower, and the hotels and restaurants. You begin to recognize the faces around town. The people are smiling and friendly and yet go about their business without undue attention to the tourists. Fellow visitors become neighbors and share stories over dinner. You become aware of the changes in the light, hard and bright under blue skies, or soft and muted under the cloud cover of a passing tropical storm. And you become conscious of the pervasive, intoxicating scent of mangoes and papayas in the air. Within a day, the warm city and the sultry weather fit comfortably, like a well-worn shirt.

The Avenida Hidalgo is the main central street, running north from the town square. It's been modestly reshaped and landscaped into a narrow mall and, like most of the streets, is well lighted at night. A stroll down Avenida Hidalgo and out along the branching byways is enough for you to get your bearings.

The town offers a great temptation to laze around in the sun on the beaches, browse leisurely through the many shops, stop for a snack and a beer at one of the many *taquerias* and restaurants, or just sit and watch children playing baseball or football (soccer) on the beach. At Playa Norte, the best place to swim at the edge of town, young, athletic travelers play volleyball and stretch out on the sand, taking breaks at the two snack bars on the beach. The streets of the village bustle with activity until siesta, when many businesses shut down for the afternoon rest. At dusk, the town jumps back to life. A heated basketball game, on the Jose Del C. Pastrana court in the *zócalo*, usually starts

up at sundown, with local teens and young adults teaming up against the tourists. Fans gather spontaneously and cheer one side or the other, taking breaks to fetch a fresh milkshake from the corner ice cream stand or a cold drink from the supermarket across the square, next to the movie house.

As night falls, the town begins to shimmer with increased activity under the bright streetlights. People line up at the pushcarts in front of the supermarket to buy fresh fruit. Children play in the streets and in the broad plaza in front of the Teatro del Puebla. A net is strung across the court, and volleyball replaces basketball as the sports attraction. Tourists, relaxed and contented from a hearty dinner, wander slowly through the shops. Occasionally, a band sets up its equipment and plays popular Caribbean music from the steps of the municipal building.

But the pleasures of Isla Mujeres extend far beyond the town. With the early rise of the tropical sun, a whole different landscape of adventures unfolds. Although it's not out of the question to walk, and while taxis are very cheap, the fun way to explore the island is on a motorbike, which can be rented from several locations for less than $10 a day. A short loop around the northern end takes you to Playa Los Cocos—the best swimming beach—and to the lagoon near the El Presidente. The two-lane road south along the western shoreline, the "Garrafón Highway," leads past the small army base and the Makas Lagoon. The island's other main swimming beach, Playa Lancheros, is just off the road, with shady palapas shelters, a snack stand, and wooden pens for sea turtles.

Near Playa Lancheros is the decaying estate of the nineteenth-century slave trader, Fermin Mundaca. The pirate built his fortress on Isla Mujeres in the mid-1800s, creating his own paradise of grand buildings and gardens. All that remain of his lush Hacienda de la Huerta (Estate of the Happy Orchard) are shady yet evocative ruins.

Farther south is the island's most wondrous natural resource, El Garrafón. Here, the combination of a large coral reef and exceptionally clear, gentle water provides hours of dazzling snorkeling. The beach is set up as a park, with a nominal entry fee, and is geared for heavy tourist traffic. A restaurant, an aquarium/museum, hamburger and ice cream stands, shops with clothes, curios, and snorkel equipment rentals are scattered across the terraced hillside. And large numbers of tourists are boated in daily from Cancún. But the crowd thins out in midafternoon, and the snorkeling is spectacular. Hundreds of species of fish, of every imaginable color and shape, blithely feed on the reef and swim by in enormous schools.

If you can bear to leave El Garrafón, the southern tip of the island is just a half-kilometer away. A path leads past the lighthouse to the small remains of a Mayan temple, dramatically perched on the cliff above the crashing waves. Most people return to town on the same highway, but the road loops around to the eastern coastline, where the shore is rugged and beautiful. The deserted beaches, with their heavier surf and gusty breezes, provide a chance to be alone (away from all the others who are "getting away from it all"), to comb the beach, gather shells and driftwood, and watch the waves.

Any appetite worked up during an adventurous day on Isla Mujeres can be easily satisfied. Taquerias and restaurants abound in every price range. Although what is conventionally considered "Mexican food" is available, and some of the enchiladas, *tortas*, and *chilaquiles* are quite good, the main fare of the island is grilled fresh fish, served with lime, rice, and fresh, handmade tortillas. The smaller restaurants, such as Sergio's, the Buccanero, La Mano de Dios, or Giltry, are very inexpensive, with entire meals for $2 or $3. Such larger, fancier establishments as Gomar, Ciro's, or Maria's, specializing in lobster, shrimp, conch, and turtle, are hardly bargains but provide fine service and a hint of luxury. For breakfast, the ideal setting can be found at the outdoor restaurants on the beach near the pier, where you can sit under thatched roofs and watch the boats go out.

A day or two is obviously not enough time to savor all the delights of Isla Mujeres. But the island's most attractive characteristic is the freedom it provides visitors—freedom to choose from a variety of activities and adventures, to shape their own days and nights, and to determine their own pace. Somewhere between the overdevelopment of nearby Cancún and the natural state of a desert island, Isla Mujeres waits, a crossroads, temporarily suspended in time, with almost any direction possible.

NOTEWORTHY

Snorkeling at El Garrafón: The coral reef, the remarkably clear waters, and the abundance of exotic tropical fish conspire to provide some of the most accessible and intriguing snorkeling in the Caribbean. A nominal admission fee is required for entrance to the park. Equipment rentals are available at the beach. If the area around the main channel looks crowded, enter the water near the long pier to the left.

Islay Contoy, an uninhabited island north of Isla Mujeres, has a marvelous bird sanctuary. Several entrepreneurs organize an entire day's outing that includes fishing, grilling and eating the catch, and snorkeling, with a long stopover on Contoy to observe the stunning variety of cormorants, pelicans, herons, egrets, and other birds. Scuba diving and deep-sea fishing trips can also be easily arranged.

WHERE TO STAY

Consistent with its gradual development as a tourist spot, Isla Mujeres features all kinds of accommodations, from the upscale tackiness of the towering El Presidente, which dominates a prime location on the northwest tip of the island, to a few relatively remote establishments on the western coast and dozens of small, modest hotels scattered around town. Among the latter are the Isleño, the Caracol, the Caribe Maya, and the Osorio, all costing about $20-$25 a night for a double room.

Hotel Rocamar
Ave. Nicolas Bravoy
Isla Mujeres, Quintana Roo, Mexico
Telephone: 988-2-01-01
Located on the eastern side of the island, at the corner of the town square, the Hotel Rocamar sits right on the edge of the sea. Most of the large rooms have balconies perched

virtually on top of the breakers. Although there are signs of weathering and minor disrepair, the Rocamar boasts a certain charm and is one of the island's best deals. The combination of ceiling fans and constant sea breeze keeps the rooms cool, and the roaring song of the surf lulls you to sleep at night. Rates start at about $25 double.

Posada Del Mar
Avenida Rueda Marina No.15
Isla Mujeres, Quintana Roo, Mexico
Telephone: (988) 2-00-44 and 2-02-76; fax: (988) 2-01-14
Designed for the traveler who wants a bit of luxury without the completely plastic nature of the Cancún resorts (or Isla Mujeres' own high-rise El Presidente), the Posada del Mar has forty-one rooms and bungalows (with air-conditioning or ceiling fans) spread out around its neatly maintained palm gardens and grounds. Facing the western beach, it offers such amenities as a fountain-fed swimming pool, restaurant, and patio bar. Rates start at $30 double in summer and $50 in winter.

Maria's Kankin
P.O. Box 69
77400 Isla Mujeres, Quintana Roo, Mexico
Telephone: (988) 3-14-20; fax: (988) 2-03-33
Perfect for a romantic getaway in the honeymoon spirit, Maria's Kankin is tucked into a lush setting of palms and flowering vegetation. Its pink stucco exterior adds to the charm of the terraced design. The patio bar and restaurant look out over the hotel's private beach, where there is a private pier for hotel guests. Rates start at $40 for two.

RESTAURANTS

It would take more than a week to eat your way through Isla Mujeres, so numerous and diverse are the restaurants. Using your instinct, pocketbook, and, best of all, tips from other travelers, you can make dining another branch of exploration.

Sergio's, on the east side of town, facing the town square, is an inexpensive spot for good fried fish. Its patio dining area is also a good spot to sit in the early evening for a cold drink and a snack of guacamole and chips.

The Buccanero, an open-air restaurant in the middle of town, serves excellent enchiladas, very cold soft drinks and beer, and a variety of local specialties.

Maria's Kankin is romantically situated in a classic tropical setting out of town on the western coast of the island. The outdoor dining room is nestled in palms and looks out over the water. Menus are hand-printed on woven straw mats. The dishes include local seafood (fresh live lobster a specialty) excellently prepared in Mexican and Continental styles. Although it is one of the more expensive places to eat on Isla Mujeres, it is also one of the loveliest.

El Limbo is the grottolike restaurant nestled under the Hotel Rocamar. Its decor is simple but intriguing, with a seashell motif reflected in the tile floor and walls. Windows overlook the breakers on the eastern coast. The food is very good, with different varieties of fresh seafood prepared in several local styles. Watch out for the salsa; it is fiery.

Brisas del Caribe, a thatch-roofed patio restaurant located a few steps from the ferry dock, is a perfect place for a sunrise breakfast. Fresh orange juice and delicious banana hotcakes are among the offerings.

Ciro's Lobster House is one of the two or three large restaurants in the central section of the village. Although it is tourist oriented, with a fully stocked bar and a television, many of the dishes are excellent. Lobster is the specialty, but the menu is extensive, and the soups are delicious.

FROM MY JOURNAL

As we pulled our motorbikes up to the gate at the Hacienda Gomar, three young teenaged boys approached, hauling wet burlap gunny sacks. They had just emerged from the lagoon, and their bags were full of shells. One boy pulled out a large conch shell and put its point to his pursed lips and blew. A long, moaning note drifted into the air. The other boys laughed as he handed me the shell and I blew a loud, flatulent rasp from the conch. They set a few of their prizes on the ground before us, and we picked out a beautiful tiger-striped specimen. They parted with it for about five dollars; it would sell for twelve or fifteen in town.

Today, there was no one walking along the eastern beaches, where the waves are wild and beautiful. Maybe it was the darkening sky and the smell of rain. That just seemed to make it more romantic. Tonight the ocean went crazy outside our window, making thunder against the rocks below the hotel. We opened our shutters wide to the crashing serenade.

HOW TO GET THERE

From Cancún, travel by taxi or bus to Puerto Juárez and take the passenger ferry to Isla Mujeres. With an automobile, drive to Punta Sam, three miles north of Puerto Juárez, and take the car ferry.

Isla Holbox

As you ride through the Yucatán jungle toward Chiquila, the mainland harbor nearest Isla Holbox, it's as if layers of civilization and pretense are peeled away before your eyes, preparing you for the simple fishing village island that rests an hour's boat ride across the sea. Along Highway 180, between Mérida and Puerto Juárez, the tourists zoom back and forth, heading to Chichén Itzá and Cancún, oblivious to the remote beauty to the north. But once you make the turn at the junction just west of Nuevo Xcan, the pace slackens and the quiet nature of the villages along the road takes hold.

Isla Holbox lies off the northeastern tip of the Yucatán Peninsula, surrounded by the clear blue Gulf waters. Although it is fifteen miles long and two miles across at its widest point, the island is inhabited only at the western end, where the small puebla of Holbox, with perhaps one hundred houses, is located. Its people live by grace of the sea and their own small gardens. Since few tourists ever find their way to Isla Holbox, the island offers a tranquil picture of indigenous life where the Gulf of Mexico meets the Caribbean, a life unspoiled by the crass commerce of hotels, restaurants, and curio shops. Without the lure of the typical resort town amenities and tourist attractions, Holbox challenges the visitor to creatively explore the unadorned setting and all its intrinsic beauty.

Much of the adventure is in getting there. Chiquila is within a few hours' drive of Cancún, Cobá, or Valladolid, and public buses run on a regular schedule from Highway 180, timed to meet the ferries to Isla Holbox. The paved two-lane road is good, and the sparse traffic moves briskly between the towns on the 46-mile (75-km) stretch from El Ideal to Chiquila. But as each village crops up almost rhythmically along the way, and as the jungle flora gradually changes from the dense inland growth to the lighter vegetation nearing the seashore, the scenery grows more absorbing, and you find yourself slowing down to take it all in. Each small town has its variations on the same themes. Around the houses with their thatched palapa roofs, lines of bright-colored laundry sway in the breeze—reds, purples, and yellows set off against the dark green tropical foliage. Chickens, hogs, and turkeys amble along the roadside, sometimes crossing your path at their own leisure. Children stare intently as you drive by, their faces sometimes breaking into friendly smiles as they shyly respond to a wave. Every puebla seems to have a baseball diamond and a basketball court, and such larger ones as Kantunilkin and San Angel have zócalos, or town squares, surrounded by the few necessary businesses.

At the end of the road, Chiquila appears to be little more than a few houses and a solitary boat dock with only the slightest activity between the arrivals and departures of the ferries. Be open to unforeseen circumstances. On our first attempt to reach Holbox, we arrived at Chiquila in the afternoon during an especially blustery storm. The wind was creating large whitecaps on the sea and blowing the warm, heavy rain horizontally across the pier. When the ferries arrived from Holbox, the passengers were drenched. The captain of the auto ferry decided not to chance the return trip. We opted to drive back to Cobá and return in the morning rather than brave the turbulent waves on the passenger ferry.

A large scow serves as the car ferry, able to transport two small cars or a truck, but as there is virtually no driving to do on Holbox, you can leave your car near the dock and take the passenger boat, which can carry up to fifty people inside. The captain and his mate tie the boat to the pier and assist the passengers aboard, waiting to collect the fare during the hour-long trip. You ride with the regulars who commute to work or shop on the mainland, and you are unlikely to encounter any non-Spanish-speaking travelers.

The ride is slow, rolling, and as smooth as the weather will allow. If a storm whips up, bringing the sea to a froth, the boat rocks and dips like a roller coaster. But on a calm day, the trip is easy and comfortable. As Isla Holbox comes into view, you may notice a bold swatch of pink in a lagoon off to the left. As the boat draws closer, a sudden commotion erupts and the patch of bright pink starts to scatter and rise, as the large flock of flamingos takes flight. Launching their gangly bodies into graceful motion, the exotic birds soar in great circles and land in the shallow water once the boat has passed. It's just the first glimpse of Holbox's simple but elegant natural wonders.

Where the ferry docks, a dirt road leads from the pier into the village. If you arrive in midmorning, with the sun already high in the sky, the puebla may look parched and desolate. A baseball diamond sits in disrepair off to the right. Only a few people are visible on the dusty streets, and the disembarking passengers seem to vanish mysteriously on the trek into town. But the hidden life and appeal of Holbox gradually unfold as you leave the pier.

Just fifty yards or so from the dock stands the only restaurant, the El Paso—a screened, circular patio with a palm roof. The town is comprised of only five to ten square blocks of houses, and as you walk through, you will catch glimpses of women preparing meals and doing laundry and children playing games in the small yards. Among the first things to catch your eye along the street are great piles of large conch and other shells near every house, discarded casually after the fish has been removed.

If you walk straight ahead on the road from the pier, you come quickly to the other side of the island, where the fishing boats are tied up and where a breathtaking expanse of white beach extends for a mile to the west and two miles to the east. Large pelicans and other seabirds amble along the shore or swoop overhead. Here, along the open sea and its surprisingly gentle, clear blue waters, is the chief allure of Holbox for the adventurous visitor—a beachcomber's paradise. Just a few minutes' walk down the beach takes you away from the village to where there is nothing but shallow ocean to one side and the tangled scrub of jungle to the other.

The sand is littered with millions of shells of every variety. In some places they cover the beach completely, crunching under foot as you walk along. There is perhaps no greater abundance of whelks, cockles, bubbles, lion's paws, and other shells anywhere else along the Yucatán Peninsula. The first sight of all those treasures is overwhelming, and as you walk along the shore, the realization sinks in that they are just a tiny representation of the rich and varied life in the surrounding sea. And except for a fishing boat or two, you may come across no other signs of life. At many points along the deserted beach, you can wade out a great distance into the water and cool your feet or swim.

If you arrive at Holbox in the morning, you can get in two or three hours of relaxed beachcombing before walking back to the village. The activity picks up as families prepare for their midday meals, frying the day's catch, pounding cornmeal into tortillas, and cooking up pots of beans and rice. After several hours of beachcombing, we walked back through town and encountered the ferryboat skipper on his stopover between runs. He commented on the conch shells we had picked up, reminded us of the departure time, and directed us to the restaurant, near the pier. At the El Paso, the fare is determined by what the sea has yielded to the fishermen that day. Generous portions of fish are deliciously grilled, served with a stack of fresh, warm, homemade corn tortillas. Black beans are served in a flavorful broth, with sliced hot peppers on the side. Add a cold bottle of beer, soda, or mineral water, and you could not ask for a heartier, more satisfying meal for the price (about $2).

Isla Holbox can be enjoyed for the day without much more than the few words of Spanish needed to order a meal and ask directions. A fluent command of the language will allow you greater access to the life of the island. Be sure to check the departure time of the ferry returning to Chiquila. However long you stay, the subtle magic of the remote island lingers well after you've watched the island slowly vanish behind you as the ferry takes you back to the Yucatán mainland.

WHERE TO STAY

Casa de Chiko—small, simple rooms for overnight stays can be arranged by Chiko and cost approximately $6 per night.

RESTAURANT

El Paso, near the pier, grills fish to perfection. The warm homemade corn tortillas and black beans make an inexpensive, memorable meal.

HOW TO GET THERE

Take a car or bus to the village of Chiquila, 46 miles/75 km north from Highway 180 at El Ideal. The ferry leaves Chiquila for Isla Holbox three times a day, at 8 a.m., 11:30 a.m., and 3:30 p.m., weather permitting, and makes the trip from Holbox at 6:30 a.m., 10 a.m., and 2 p.m. A private boat is 100,000 Mexican pesos (US $40) round-trip.

PRACTICAL TIPS

Immigration: Proof of U.S. citizenship and a tourist card (provided free of charge by your travel agent or airline) are required for entry to Mexico. Save the carbon copy of your tourist card to present on departure. You'll need 23,000 Mexican pesos (US$10) for the departure tax.

Currency: The Mexican peso fluctuates daily but was approximately 2,300 to US$1 at publication time.

Language: Spanish is the language, and you'll hear little else on Holbox. Some English is spoken on Isla Mujeres.

Health: Avoid tap water. Mineral water is excellent and inexpensive.

CAYMAN ISLANDS

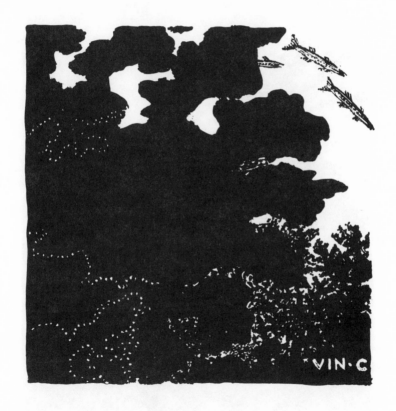

The Cayman Islands, 480 miles south of Miami, are a British Crown Colony, a friendly mix of English, Irish, Welsh, Scottish, and African. Grand Cayman, the largest, is a bustling tourist center with the highest standard of living in the Caribbean. Sister islands Little Cayman and Cayman Brac, thirty minutes away by twin-propeller plane, have changed little since Christopher Columbus first saw them in 1503. Both of these small, flat islands are actually pinnacles rising 5,000 feet from the ocean floor. In the crystal-clear water that surrounds them is some of the best scuba diving to be found anywhere in the Northern Hemisphere: cavern dives, wreck dives, wall dives, and exploration dives.

Little Cayman

"Little Cayman is the way it was and still is," says native Sam McCoy. It would be hard to imagine an island any quieter, for there are just two dozen permanent residents. More than 98 percent of the island remains uninhabited and undeveloped, and even the airport is a grass landing strip, while most of the roads are unpaved trails. Quiet paths lead into the jungle bush, alive with wildlife and birds, including boobies, iguanas, and parrots. A great salt pond is filled with a miniature version of tarpon.

The spectacular vertical walls and living coral reefs of Little Cayman are legendary among experienced divers. The sea is so clear, with no mountain runoff or pollution, that visibility averages between 125 and 200 feet year-round. The clear visibility, the extended reefs, and the abundant marine life provide ultimate diving and snorkeling for the traveler seeking a quiet, unspoiled island retreat.

NOTEWORTHY

Bloody Bay Marine Park: A dive beneath the ocean's mirror-smooth surface into Bloody Bay Marine Park is a voyage into the third dimension, a world of lush coral gardens, giant sponges, trees of black coral, elaborate sea fans, and majestic eagle rays. The park teems with life: yellowtails, sergeant majors, angelfish, green morays, tarpons, octopuses, and silversides as well as semitame grouper, jewfish, and eels that allow close inspection. At one place along Bloody Bay Wall, the drop-off begins in 18 feet of water and plummets vertically to 1,200 feet. This may be the most beautiful dive spot in the Caribbean!

Spear guns are prohibited, and no type of marine life of any kind can be taken from the park. Access is limited, and only certain dive operations licensed by the Marine Conservation Board may bring divers.

Spring to fall is the best bet for diving here. During the winter, strong prevailing northeasterlies mean that glassy-

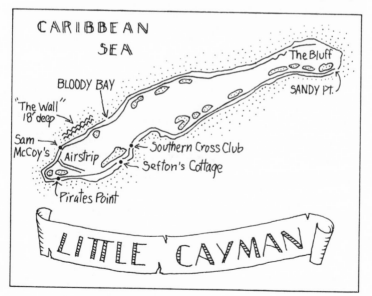

smooth seas are uncommon, although underwater visibility is still good in all seasons.

WHERE TO STAY

Pirates Point Resort
Little Cayman, British West Indies
Telephone: 1-809-948-4210
Gladys Howard is owner-manager of this six-room diving resort located on five beachfront acres. An avid diver and *cordon bleu* chef, Gladys provides a friendly, hospitable second home for her guests. "My guests set their own schedules for diving and fishing," she says, "and the kitchen never closes." In summer, rates are $185 single and $290 per couple; $320 in winter. Rates include all meals, wine, trips to reefs, tanks and diving equipment, bicycles, and transportation to the airport.

Southern Cross Club
Little Cayman, British West Indies
Telephone: 1-809-948-3255
There are five duplex bungalows at this casual beachfront hotel. Everything is run family-style; there are no keys to the rooms (crime is unknown on the island), and the bar is run on a do-it-yourself system with honor tab. Bicycles and windsurfing equipment are provided, and a dive master is there to rent equipment and arrange trips to the reefs. In summer, rates run $105 single and $180 per couple with three meals included.

Sam McCoy's Diving and Fishing Lodge
Little Cayman, British West Indies
Telephone: 1-809-948-2249
c/o in the U.S.A.
631 Cochran Dr.
Greensburg, PA 15601
Telephone: 1-800-843-2177
or 412-834-4064 in Pennsylvania
Mary and Sam McCoy are native to the Caymans, and their six-room lodge is a family-run business. Daily rates from $135 single and $250 per couple include three meals, all diving, and transportation.

Leonie's Guest House
Blossom Village, Little Cayman, British West Indies
No telephone
Very basic rooms are sometimes available (when not in use by locals) for $25 per person including meals.

Sefton's Cottage
Box 681
Grand Cayman, British West Indies
Telephone: 7-4144 on Grand Cayman,
8-3255 on Little Cayman
Near the Southern Cross Club, Nancy and Ron Sefton's two-bedroom beachfront house rents by the day or week. Also available is a one-bedroom apartment.

RESTAURANTS

The only food on Little Cayman is served at your guest house or hotel.

HOW TO GET THERE

Cayman Airways operates flights daily except Tuesday and Thursday from Grand Cayman and Cayman Brac, and flying time is approximately 30 minutes.

Cayman Brac

The incredible clarity of the aquamarine sea and the light bouncing off the white sand through crystal-clear water is the overwhelming first impression of Cayman Brac as the twin-propeller plane lands from thriving Grand Cayman.

Twelve miles long and an average of 1.5 miles wide, the island has 1,300 residents, most of whom live along the north coast where the island's distinctive old Brac houses, schools, church, and museum are located. The south coast is virtually unchanged natural landscape, home to scores of bird and plant species.

The most striking feature on the island is the bluff ("brac" in Gaelic), a formidable geological formation riddled with over 100 caves, including Rebekah's Cave, Bat's Cave, Great Cave, and Cliff Cave. Steps have been carved in the side of the brac at a point in Spot Bay, and the walk to the plateau at the top is well worth the effort for the views along the way. Boobies with long pointed wings whirl and swoop from the bluff to the sea and back.

The bluff yields veins of caymanite, a semiprecious gemstone found only in the Cayman Islands. It is a protected natural resource, and only two islanders are licensed to extract it. The color streaks dictate the form as pieces are cut and polished for distinctive jewelry.

Cayman Brac has superb shore diving as well as boat diving, and there are more than forty excellent dive sites, with more being discovered every year. The majority of them are at the western end of the island, making the boat rides from the two dive resorts quick and convenient. Both sides of the Brac offer excellent diving, including awesome drop-offs, unique underwater attractions, and high-quality, shallow/medium-depth coral gardens.

NOTEWORTHY

The Hobbit is a drop-off less than a quarter-mile east of the Tiara Beach Resort. Named after the classic by J. R. R. Tolkien, the drop-off has a fairyland appearance that features a number of giant, bizarre-looking sponges. Fish life here is extremely active and includes blue runner jacks, barracudas, and ocean triggerfish.

WHERE TO STAY

Divi Tiara Beach Hotel
Cayman Brac, British West Indies
Telephone: (809) 948-7553; U.S.: (800) 367-3484
Fax: (607) 277-3624
This modern beachfront resort—one of two hotels in operation on the island—is considered the largest and most successful dedicated dive resort in the Cayman Islands. Rooms are air-conditioned but also have ceiling fans. There

are tennis courts, a swimming pool, and diving and windsurfing equipment; underwater photo classes are also available. Single rooms start at $75 in summer and $85 per couple, increasing to $120 for one or two in winter.

Brac Reef Beach Resort
P.O. Box 235 West End
Cayman Brac, British West Indies
Telephone: (800) 948-7323; U.S. (800) 327-3835
Fax: (800) 948-7207
Less than 150 yards east of Divi Tiara, the Brac Reef Beach Resort is another dedicated diving resort with forty comfortable, modern rooms facing the beach and a breezy two-

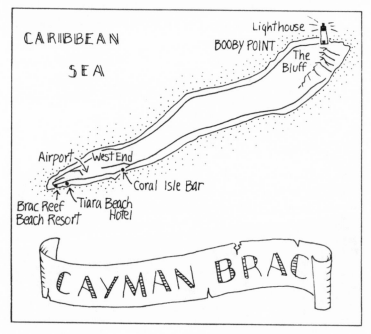

story gazebo-bar at the end of a jetty. A freshwater pool and Jacuzzi face the long stretch of white sand that slopes toward the sea. Rates start at $69 single, $79 per couple in low season and $79 single and $99 per couple for winter. Meal and dive packages are available. Adjacent to the hotel is the headquarters of Brac Aquatics, the Brac's oldest and best-known dive operation.

HOUSES TO RENT

A three-bedroom house in the center of the island is available for rent at $105 per day per couple. Reserve with Jim Walden, Sunburst, Route 1, Box 723, Joseph, OR 97846.

A small, unadorned "cottage" (looking more like a trailer) is on the water's edge next to the Coral Isle bar and rents for $100 a week. Reserve with Otly Scott, Cayman Brac, British West Indies.

RESTAURANTS

There are a variety of restaurants, including Blackies, off South Side; La Esperanza, at Creek; Ed's Place, at West End; Suahil, at Spot Bay; and Watering Place, at Watering Place.

HOW TO GET THERE

Cayman Airways has nonstop service from Houston, Memphis, Atlanta, Miami, and Tampa to Grand Cayman, as well as service to Cayman Brac from Miami (just one hour flying time). Northwest, the pioneer nonsmoking airline, flies from Memphis and Miami with connecting flights to other U.S. cities.

From Grand Cayman, Cayman Airways has a twin-propeller commuter aircraft that flies daily to Cayman Brac. The same aircraft goes on to Little Cayman daily except Tuesday and Thursday.

PRACTICAL TIPS

Immigration: A passport or other proof of U.S. citizenship and a return or ongoing ticket are needed for entrance to the Cayman Islands. The departure tax is $7.50.

Currency: The local currency is the Cayman dollar with a fixed exchange rate at CI$1 = US$1.20. (However, restaurants and shops will convert at US$1.25 in order to cover bank charges.)

Reconfirmation: Once you have landed in the Caymans, it is extremely important to reconfirm your return reservations seventy-two hours (3 days) in advance. This is easiest to do on arrival while the airport is open.

Drugs: The Cayman Islands have the severest antidrug laws in the Caribbean. Violators (marijuana included) are immediately arrested and taken off to jail.

BRITISH VIRGIN ISLANDS

We found some of the most beautiful islands in the Caribbean in the British Virgin Islands: the finest white sand beaches, the most luminescent sea, excellent snorkeling, friendly English-speaking inhabitants, and thoughtful controls on development.

Unlike the American Virgin Islands just a few miles to the south, the BVIs, as they are most often called, have no casinos, no slick condominiums or dozens of cruise ships docking regularly with thousands of daytime passengers. Even the largest and most populated BVI has yet to install a traffic light. Life moves quietly and gently in these beautiful islands.

Most of the fifty-one British Virgin Islands are small and uninhabited, a veritable sailor's paradise of quiet bays, beaches, and goat trails for hiking. Two of the largest BVIs, Tortola and Virgin Gorda, are too well visited by smart travelers to be called undiscovered. Tortola, the largest island (attached to Beef Island by a bridge), is known for its long, uncrowded beaches, fine local restaurants, and warm hospitality. There are no high-rises on Tortola, no traffic jams, and no frantic pace.

Virgin Gorda is famous for its three outstanding luxury resorts—Little Dix Bay, Biras Creek, and Bitter End—and for its travel-poster-familiar rock formations that provide pools for swimming and snorkeling. We preferred Olde Yard Inn for its cuisine and good library and the eight-room-two-villa Drake's Anchorage for its secluded location on tiny (125 acres), privately owned Mosquito Island, 100 yards off mainland Virgin Gorda.

After visiting all the inhabited BVIs, three stand out as unique and undiscovered: Anegada, Jost Van Dyke, and Guana.

Anegada

The fifteen-minute flight in an eight-seater plane from Beef Island (Tortola) passes over no other island; you arrive on this large, flat island feeling you've reached the edge of the world. Goats graze contentedly near the runway, and it is immediately apparent that the island is mostly untrammeled and open land. The twelve-mile north shore is almost one unbroken stretch of shimmering white sand surrounded by coral reef. With an island population of 150 and a maximum (hardly ever attained) visitor capacity of thirty-six, we calculated that if everyone went to the beach at the same time, it would still look deserted.

Conch fishing and boat building are the main occupations for the islanders. At "The Settlement," which is almost too small and dispersed to be called a town, there are piles of white conch shells just offshore where the fishing boats tie up. The Presbyterian church and the cricket field (teams from other islands come occasionally) are the focal points of island life. If you are here on Sunday, the church is well worth visiting to hear the fine voices and to meet local inhabitants as they come to greet their fellow island neighbors.

Anegada is an island for beach lovers, those who enjoy walking endlessly along a deserted beach, snorkeling in a quiet sea, and swimming in water that is warm and translucent. It is an island for hikers who like tranquil walks far from the noise and pollution of automobiles and motorbikes and for readers who will rejoice in the peace, solitude, and unhurried existence of an island in time.

NOTEWORTHY

The Anegada Reef has claimed over 300 ships since the age of exploration and is now a diver's paradise. Fish life is abundant, and the wreckage of vessels is easily seen. Within the wreck of *The Rochus*, an incredible array of fish life can be seen.

WHERE TO STAY

Anegada Reef Hotel
Anegada, British Virgin Islands
Telephone: (809) 495-8002
Anegada Reef Hotel is the only place to rent a room on the island. The twelve rooms have recently been improved with small, trellised verandas, air-conditioning, private baths, and hot water. Wall-to-wall carpeting and other non-Caribbean furnishings seem intended to reassure visitors that they are safely in the hands of a "civilized" establishment. At the open-air dining room and bar, visitors can enjoy the local specialties, including lobster and conch, while watching the horizon for sailboats, which regularly drop anchor for lunch. The white sand beach extends for

miles in each direction. Rates include meals (but not 12% service and 7% tax) and are $80 per person in summer and $90 in winter. Package dive tours and introductory scuba diving lessons are available. The hotel owns a fully equipped 31-foot Bertram for deep-sea fishing.

Neptune's Treasure (Anegada Beach Campground)

The Settlement, Anegada, British Virgin Islands
Telephone: (809) 495-8038
Neptune's Treasure, a five-minute walk along the beach from Anegada Reef Hotel, is an excellent restaurant that serves breakfast, lunch, and dinner to people who moor their boats offshore. Although there are no rooms, they will provide 8' x 10' and 10' x 12' tents and allow you to use the restaurant toilet, which has an outdoor hose for showering. If you bring your own tent, there is a nominal charge for use of the site.

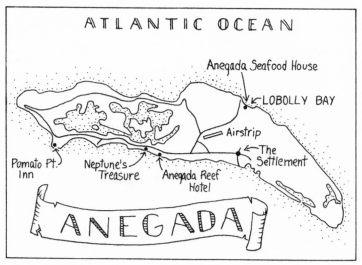

RESTAURANTS

Del's Restaurant and Bar in The Settlement is a full-service restaurant that serves West Indian-style food daily for breakfast, lunch, and dinner.

At Anegada Seafood House in Loblolly Bay, Diane and Aubrey, West Indians from Trinidad, serve delicious food (especially the conch stew) in their open-air restaurant that faces a stretch of white sand.

Neptune's Treasure is run by the friendly Soares family, who came from Bermuda as commercial fishermen over twenty years ago. Neptune's provides the island's freshest fish and lobster. You can order from the menu ($12-$25) or what they call "home cooking," which costs US$6 and usually includes fresh fish, vegetables, and salad. Open seven days a week.

Pomato Point Beach Restaurant, overlooking a spectacular beach, offers a relaxed and comfortable atmo-

sphere, but alas, it is not always open. Local dishes are served for lunch and dinner: conch, barbecued lobster, and other local seafoods.

HOW TO GET THERE

Air BVI flies from Beef Island-Tortola on Monday, Wednesday, Friday, and Sunday. On Tuesday, Speedy's ferry operates between Tortola, Virgin Gorda, and Anegada. Telephone (809) 495-5240 (or on Tortola, 5-5240/5-5235) for schedule information.

Jost Van Dyke

Jost (rhymes with toast) Van Dyke is a mere twenty-minute ferry ride from Tortola's West End, yet the island remains a supremely tranquil setting for anyone seeking a stress-free vacation without automobiles in a setting of exquisite beauty. There are approximately 130 very gracious and hospitable inhabitants.

Arrival from Tortola is at Great Harbour. Verdant hills with flamboyant trees cascade gently down to one of the most perfect beaches we've seen in the Caribbean. Offshore, sailing yachts anchor in clear turquoise water. Two restaurant-bars, a bakery stand, and a small hotel welcome visitors with all the comforts and provisions necessary to make this island the ultimate undiscovered getaway.

To explore the island, there are only two choices: by foot or by boat. The walk over the hill from Great Harbour to White Bay is not long, and the views are breathtaking. The beach at White Bay is perfection. Along the stretch of fine white sand there are only two houses and a four-cottage hotel. As we swam in the calm, limpid water, a dozen pelicans were our only companions. The local inhabitants are happy to arrange a boat for the return trip or for further exploration to Little Harbour.

WHERE TO STAY

Rudy's Mariner Inn

Great Harbour, Jost Van Dyke, British Virgin Islands
Telephone: (809) 775-3588
Rudy's three-room hotel has kitchenettes, a beach bar and
restaurant, dining patio, and a grocery store. It is very convenient to the ferry landing and nearby nature trails. Rates
start at $55 in the summer and $75 in the winter.

Sandcastle Hotel

White Bay, Jost Van Dyke, British Virgin Islands
Telephone: (803) 237-8900
U.S.A. mailing address:

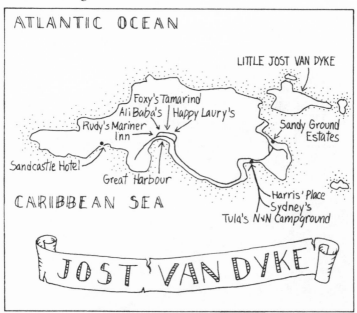

P.O. Box 540
Pawleys Island, SC 29585
Telephone: (803) 237-8900; fax: (803) 237-8903
This four-beachfront-cottage hotel is located on one of the most beautiful beaches in the Caribbean. Comfortable and tasteful appointments give an air of luxury, but all lighting is by propane lanterns, and showers are outdoors. The restaurant serves gourmet cuisine. (The Culinary Institute of America holds a five-day course at the hotel in island cooking.) Windsurfing, snorkeling equipment, and a Day Sailer are available. Rates include three meals and are $235 per day for two in off-season and $295 per day in winter.

Sandy Ground Estates
P.O. Box 594
West End, Tortola, British Virgin Islands
Telephone: (809) 494-3391

Sandy Ground Estates has eight separate, secluded villas with fully equipped kitchens, each located a short walk from the 800-foot-long private beach. Summer rates are $750 per week, winter $950.

Harris' Place
Little Harbour, Jost Van Dyke, British Virgin Islands
Telephone: (809) 774-0774
Harris has two basic rooms to rent for $45-$55 in summer and $50-$65 in winter. There is live reggae music Tuesday and Thursday.

Tula's N & N Campground
Little Harbour, Jost Van Dyke, British Virgin Islands
Telephone: (809) 774-0744 or 775-3073
Tula's is on the water's edge; a grocery, restaurant, and snack bar are conveniently nearby. This pleasant campsite charges $25 to $35 for 8' x 10' and 9' x 12' tents, $10 for a tent site, and $4 per person for a bare site in summer.

RESTAURANTS

Sydney's: This beach bar and restaurant in Little Harbour serves fresh boiled lobster, fish, conch, spareribs, and chicken for lunch or dinner. There is a pig roast every Monday and Saturday night in season.

Ali Baba's, in Great Harbour, is run by Baba Hatchett. The cuisine is West Indian, the drinks are tropical (including Baba's special rum punch), and the atmosphere is casual and friendly. Located west of the customs house, Ali Baba's is open for breakfast, lunch, and dinner. (Make your dinner reservations by 6 p.m.)

Foxy's Tamarind, in Great Harbour, serves dinner six nights a week featuring specialties such as Rummy Raisin Chicken and grilled local fish, all served "family style." Reservations are requested before 5 p.m. Ask about the live calypso music night.

Happy Laury's, located near the main dock on the beach at Great Harbour, specializes in conch fritters, fish, chicken, and chips. The bar is known for a local house drink special, The Happy Laury Pain Killer, and there is occasional live music by Reuben Chinnery and the Roots.

Harris' Place is located on the water's edge at Little Harbour and is open seven days a week for breakfast, lunch, and dinner. Harris offers a no-wait lunch program. Menu includes lobster, fish, chicken, conch, hamburgers, sandwiches, conch fritters, and other West Indian dishes.

Rudy's Mariner's Rendezvous, tucked into the western end of Great Harbour, specializes in lobster and local fish. Rudy's is open for dinner until 1 a.m. Make reservations in person at the customs office.

Sandcastle White Bay offers romantic candlelight dining on a beautiful white sand beach. Lunch is served at 1:30 p.m. and dinner at 7:30 p.m. Dinner entrées include rack of lamb, duck a l'orange, and stuffed grouper. Dress is informal; reservations are required.

HOW TO GET THERE

There is no plane service. Reel World Ferry (tel. 809-494-3450) operates daily between West End, Tortola, and Jost Van Dyke. (Departs Tortola at 9:30 a.m. and 4:15 p.m., return to Tortola at 7:45 a.m. and 2:30 p.m.) The crossing time is approximately twenty minutes and costs $9 round-trip.

Guana Island

Although Guana Island is completely owned by the Guana Island Club, it is so unspoiled and of such interest to nature lovers that we've included it as one of our favorite BVIs. The approach to Guana's dock gives the first hint of the island's 850-acre privacy; there's not a sign of civilization, only a verdant island alive with exotic birds. The rock formation on the point looks like the head of an iguana and gives the island its name.

Ardent conservationist Henry Jarecki purchased the island in 1975 and limits guests to a maximum of thirty at any one time. No homes or condominiums are allowed. There are no other man-made structures beyond the small lodge set on a breeze-swept hill. Guana is a wildlife sanctuary, where lucky zoologists and botanists come to study the native flora and fauna. Rare roseate flamingos have been reintroduced to the pond and are now the only ones living in the BVIs. Black-necked stilts, herons, egrets, the endangered masked booby, frigate birds, and the rare bridled quail dove are but a few of the over fifty species of birds which can be regularly observed on the island.

The miles of trails around the island are lined with

orchids, jasmine, frangipani, flamboyant, plumeria, oleander, hibiscus, agave, and other native succulents. In the orchard, fresh fruit is picked daily from trees of papaya, mango, orange, grapefruit, lemon, lime, banana, avocado, pineapple, and breadfruit.

There are seven deserted beaches, some for sunning and swimming, some for snorkeling, and two so remote you can reach them only by boat. Beneath the pristine surface of the water are 125 species of colorful reef fish.

Guana Island Club
Box 32, Road Town, Tortola, British Virgin Islands
Telephone: (809) 494-2354
These native stone cottages were built on the historic ruins of a centuries-old Quaker estate, which was once a sugar-cane plantation. The fifteen rooms are charming and comfortable. Meals in the central clubhouse feature home-

baked breads and island-grown fruits and vegetables. Tennis, croquet, sailing, windsurfing, deep-sea fishing, sunset cruises, and castaway picnics are available. Rates start at $275 per couple in off-season and $465 in peak winter season and include all meals. The island's beaches and trails are limited to hotel guests only.

HOW TO GET THERE

Guana's boat will meet you at Beef Island (Tortola) Airport for the ten-minute ride.

PRACTICAL TIPS

Immigration: Visitors are welcome in the British Virgin Islands, provided they possess return (or ongoing) tickets. A passport is the principal requirement for entry into the BVIs. For U.S. and Canadian citizens, an authenticated birth certificate or voter's registration card will suffice. There is a $5 departure tax when leaving by air, and $3 by sea.

Currency: BVI currency is the U.S. dollar.

Language: British English with a friendly West Indian accent.

Epilogue

Island enthusiasts take note: there are many more un-discovered islands not included in this book. This was especially true in the seemingly endless chain of Family Islands in the Bahamas. Beyond Exuma and Long Island lie such hideaways as Farmer's Cay, Crooked Island, Acklins, the Jumento Cays (Ragged Island, Flamingo Cay, Nurse Cay), and Mayaguana Island—with a four-room Sheraton!

Although listed in some guidebooks as an uninhabited "guano island," Isla Los Roques, in the Caribbean about seventy-five miles north of Caracas, was consistently recommended by native Venezuelans for its beautiful clear waters and gorgeous beaches. It supports a small fishing village, is accessible by small plane, and remains essentially undiscovered by most non-Venezuelans: a truly secluded hideaway for the adventurous traveler.

The footloose traveler might also explore the hundreds of islands around the coast of Cuba, from the large Isla de Pinos to the many small cays of the Sabana Archipelago. Off Haitian shores, Île de la Tortue, Île de la Gonave, Isla Beata, and Isla Saona await their first visitors.

The Caribbean stretches westward to the Central

American coast as well, encompassing the Bay Islands off Honduras and the Corn Islands off Nicaragua, and far to the south it shimmers along the beaches of Colombia's San Andrés-Providencia Islands. Panama's exotic San Blas Islands are well worth visiting for their colorful matriarchal Indian culture and beautiful beaches.

Enchanted islands sometimes appear where you least expect them. During several visits to Marie-Galante and Les Saintes in the French West Indies, I bypassed islands that guidebooks described as "flat, barren, and uninhabited." But when I later ventured forth on my own, I was surprised to find a little jewel off Guadeloupe: an ancient south Atlantic mountain rising from the sea. I was entranced by an eighteenth-century village, wonderful beaches, and fine French cuisine.

The Caribbean harbors many more such opportunities for discovery and exploration for the intrepid traveler willing to make the extra effort. The more challenging the journey, the greater the rewards of secluded destinations with undiscovered charms and hidden beauty.

Photo credits: Kate Butler (D. Donne Bryant Stock), Clayton Call, V.L. Costa, Michael Doneff, Karen Weiner Escalera, Robert Fried, Marc Garanger, Gerald Marella (D. Donne Bryant Stock), Joe Petrocik, Derek Richardson, Mary Shapiro, Burl Willes

Other Books from John Muir Publications

Adventure Vacations: From Trekking in New Guinea to Swimming in Siberia, Bangs 256 pp. $17.95

Asia Through the Back Door, 3rd ed., Steves and Gottberg 326 pp. $15.95

Belize: A Natural Destination, Mahler and Wotkyns 312 pp. $16.95 (avail. 9/91)

Buddhist America: Centers, Retreats, Practices, Morreale 400 pp. $12.95

Bus Touring: Charter Vacations, U.S.A., Warren with Bloch 168 pp. $9.95

California Public Gardens: A Visitor's Guide, Sigg 304 pp. $16.95

Catholic America: Self-Renewal Centers and Retreats, Christian-Meyer 325 pp. $13.95

Complete Guide to Bed & Breakfasts, Inns & Guesthouses, 1991-92, Lanier 520 pp. $16.95

Costa Rica: A Natural Destination, Sheck 280 pp. $15.95

Elderhostels: The Students' Choice, 2nd ed., Hyman 304 pp. $15.95

Environmental Vacations: Volunteer Projects to Save the Planet, Ocko 240 pp. $15.95

Europe 101: History & Art for the Traveler, 4th ed., Steves and Openshaw 372 pp. $15.95

Europe Through the Back Door, 9th ed., Steves 432 pp. $16.95

Floating Vacations: River, Lake, and Ocean Adventures, White 256 pp. $17.95

Great Cities of Eastern Europe, Rapoport 256 pp. $15.95 (avail. 11/91)

Gypsying After 40: A Guide to Adventure and Self-Discovery, Harris 264 pp. $14.95

The Heart of Jerusalem, Nellhaus 336 pp. $12.95

Indian America: A Traveler's Companion, 2nd ed., Eagle/Walking Turtle 448 pp. $17.95

Mona Winks: Self-Guided Tours of Europe's Top Museums, Steves and Openshaw 456 pp. $14.95

Opera! The Guide to Western Europe's Great Houses, Zietz 280 pp. $18.95

Paintbrushes and Pistols: How the Taos Artists Sold the West, Taggett and Schwarz 280 pp. $17.95

The People's Guide to Mexico, 8th ed., Franz 608 pp. $17.95

The People's Guide to RV Camping in Mexico, Franz with Rogers 320 pp. $13.95

Ranch Vacations: The Complete Guide to Guest and Resort, Fly-Fishing, and Cross-Country Skiing Ranches, 2nd ed., Kilgore 396 pp. $18.95

The Shopper's Guide to Art and Crafts in the Hawaiian Islands, Schuchter 272 pp. $13.95

The Shopper's Guide to Mexico, Rogers and Rosa 224 pp. $9.95

The Shopper's Guide to Art and Crafts in the Hawaiian Islands, Schuchter 272 pp. $13.95

The Shopper's Guide to Mexico, Rogers and Rosa 224 pp. $9.95

Ski Tech's Guide to Equipment, Skiwear, and Accessories, edited by Tanler 144 pp. $11.95

Ski Tech's Guide to Maintenance and Repair, edited by Tanler 160 pp. $11.95

A Traveler's Guide to Asian Culture, Chambers 224 pp. $13.95

Traveler's Guide to Healing Centers and Retreats in North America, Rudee and Blease 240 pp. $11.95

Understanding Europeans, Miller 272 pp. $14.95

Undiscovered Islands of the Caribbean, 2nd ed., Willes 232 pp. $14.95

Undiscovered Islands of the Mediterranean, Moyer and Willes 232 pp. $14.95

Undiscovered Islands of the U.S. and Canadian West Coast, Moyer and Willes 256 pp. $15.95

A Viewer's Guide to Art: A Glossary of Gods, People, and Creatures, Shaw and Warren 152 pp. $10.95

2 to 22 Days Series
These pocket-size itineraries (4½″ × 8″) are a refreshing departure from ordinary guidebooks. Each offers 22 flexible daily itineraries that can be used to get the most out of vacations of any length. Included are not only "must see" attractions but also little-known villages and hidden "jewels" as well as valuable general information.

22 Days Around the World, 1992 ed., Rapoport and Willes 256 pp. $12.95

2 to 22 Days Around the Great Lakes, 1991 ed., Schuchter 176 pp. $9.95

22 Days in Alaska, Lanier 128 pp. $7.95

22 Days in the American Southwest, 2nd ed., Harris 176 pp. $9.95

2 to 22 Days in Asia, 1992 ed., Rapoport and Willes 176 pp. $9.95

2 to 22 Days in Australia, 1992 ed., Gottberg 192 pp. $9.95

22 Days in California, 2nd ed., Rapoport 176 pp. $9.95

22 Days in China, Duke and Victor 144 pp. $7.95

22 Days in Europe, 5th ed., Steves 192 pp. $9.95

2 to 22 Days in Florida, 1992 ed., Harris 192 pp. $9.95

2 to 22 Days in France, 1991 ed., Steves 192 pp. $9.95

22 Days in Germany, Austria & Switzerland, 3rd ed., Steves 136 pp. $7.95

2 to 22 Days in Great Britain, 1991 ed., Steves 192 pp. $9.95

2 to 22 Days in Hawaii, 1992 ed., Schuchter 176 pp. $9.95

22 Days in India, Mathur 136 pp. $7.95

22 Days in Japan, Old 136 pp. $7.95

22 Days in Mexico, 2nd ed., Rogers and Rosa 128 pp. $7.95

2 to 22 Days in New England, 1991 ed., Wright 176 pp. $9.95

2 to 22 Days in New Zealand, 1991 ed., Schuchter 176 pp. $9.95

2 to 22 Days in Norway, Sweden, & Denmark, 1991 ed., Steves 184 pp. $9.95

2 to 22 Days in the Pacific Northwest, 1991 ed., Harris 184 pp. $9.95

22 Days in the Rockies, Rapoport 176 pp. $9.95

22 Days in Spain & Portugal, 3rd ed., Steves $7.95

22 Days in Texas, Harris 176 pp. $9.95

22 Days in Thailand, Richardson 176 pp. $9.95

22 Days in the West Indies, Morreale and Morreale 136 pp. $7.95

Parenting Series

Being a Father: Family, Work, and Self, *Mothering* Magazine 176 pp. $12.95

Preconception: A Woman's Guide to Preparing for Pregnancy and Parenthood, Aikey-Keller 232 pp. $14.95

Schooling at Home: Parents, Kids, and Learning, *Mothering* Magazine 264 pp. $14.95

Teens: A Fresh Look, *Mothering* Magazine 240 pp. $14.95

"Kidding Around" Travel Guides for Young Readers

Written for kids eight years of age and older. Generously illustrated in two colors with imaginative characters and images. An adventure to read and a treasure to keep.

Kidding Around Atlanta, Pedersen 64 pp. $9.95

Kidding Around Boston, Byers 64 pp. $9.95

Kidding Around Chicago, Davis 64 pp. $9.95

Kidding Around the Hawaiian Islands, Lovett 64 pp. $9.95

Kidding Around London, Lovett 64 pp. $9.95

Kidding Around Los Angeles, Cash 64 pp. $9.95

Kidding Around the National Parks of the Southwest, Lovett 108 pp. $12.95

Kidding Around New York City, Lovett 64 pp. $9.95

Kidding Around Paris, Clay 64 pp. $9.95

Kidding Around Philadelphia, Clay 64 pp. $9.95

Kidding Around San Diego, Luhrs 64 pp. $9.95 (avail. 9/91)

Kidding Around San Francisco, Zibart 64 pp. $9.95

Kidding Around Santa Fe, York 64 pp. $9.95

Kidding Around Seattle, Steves 64 pp. $9.95

Kidding Around Spain, Biggs 108 pp. $12.95 (avail. 9/91)

Kidding Around Washington, D.C., Pedersen 64 pp. $9.95

Environmental Books for Young Readers

Written for kids eight years and older. Examines the environmental issues and opportunities that today's kids will face during their lives.

The Indian Way: Learning to Communicate with Mother Earth, McLain 114 pp. $9.95

The Kids' Environment Book: What's Awry and Why, Pedersen 192 pp. $13.95

Rads, Ergs, and Cheeseburgers: The Kids' Guide to Energy and the Environment, Yanda 108 pp. $12.95

"Extremely Weird" Series for Young Readers

Written for kids eight years of age and older. Designed to help kids appreciate the world around them. Each book includes full-color photographs with detailed and entertaining descriptions.

Extremely Weird Bats, Lovett 48 pp. $9.95 paper

Extremely Weird Frogs, Lovett 48 pp. $9.95 paper

Extremely Weird Primates, Lovett 48 pp. $9.95 paper (avail. 9/91)

Extremely Weird Reptiles, Lovett 48 pp. $9.95 paper (avail. 9/91)
Extremely Weird Spiders, Lovett 48 pp. $9.95 paper

Quill Hedgehog Adventures Series

Written for kids eight years of age and older. Our new series of green fiction for kids follows the adventures of Quill Hedgehog and his Animalfolk friends.

Quill's Adventures in the Great Beyond, Book 1, Waddington-Feather 96 pp. $5.95 (avail. 9/91)
Quill's Adventures in Wasteland, Book 2, Waddington-Feather 132 pp. $5.95 (avail. 9/91)
Quill's Adventures in Grozzieland, Book 3, Waddington-Feather 132 pp. $5.95 (avail. 9/91)

Other Young Readers Titles

Kids Explore America's Hispanic Heritage, edited by Cozzens 112 pp. $7.95 (avail. 11/91)

Automotive Repair Manuals

How to Keep Your VW Alive, 14th ed., 440 pp. $21.95
How to Keep Your Subaru Alive 480 pp. $21.95
How to Keep Your Toyota Pickup Alive 392 pp. $21.95
How to Keep Your Datsun/Nissan Alive 544 pp. $21.95

Other Automotive Books

The Greaseless Guide to Car Care Confidence: Take the Terror Out of Talking to Your Mechanic, Jackson 224 pp. $14.95

Off-Road Emergency Repair & Survival, Ristow 160 pp. $9.95

Ordering Information

If you cannot find our books in your local bookstore, you can order directly from us. Please check the "Available" date above. If you send us money for a book not yet available, we will hold your money until we can ship you the book. Your books will be sent to you via UPS (for U.S. destinations). UPS will not deliver to a P.O. Box; please give us a street address. Include $2.75 for the first item ordered and $.50 for each additional item to cover shipping and handling costs. For airmail within the U.S., enclose $4.00. All foreign orders will be shipped surface rate; please enclose $3.00 for the first item and $1.00 for each additional item. Please inquire about foreign airmail rates.

Method of Payment

Your order may be paid by check, money order, or credit card. We cannot be responsible for cash sent through the mail. All payments must be made in U.S. dollars drawn on a U.S. bank. Canadian postal money orders in U.S. dollars are acceptable. For VISA, MasterCard, or American Express orders, include your card number, expiration date, and your signature, or call (800) 888-7504. Books ordered on American Express cards can be shipped only to the billing address of the cardholder. Sorry, no C.O.D.'s. Residents of sunny New Mexico, add 5.875% tax to the total.

Address all orders and inquiries to:
John Muir Publications
P.O. Box 613
Santa Fe, NM 87504
(505) 982-4078
(800) 888-7504